COMPREHENSION AND GRAMMAR

YEAR 3

PASCAL PRESS

CONTENTS

Term 1

Fiction Unit
Lexile Levels 560L–640L

Nonfiction Unit
Lexile Levels 630L–710L

Term 2

Fiction Unit
Lexile Levels 620L–660L

Nonfiction Unit
Lexile Levels 680L–720L

Term 3

Fiction Unit

Lexile Levels 640L–700L

Nonfiction Unit

Lexile Levels 700L–740L

Term 4

Fiction Unit

Lexile Levels 690L–780L

Nonfiction Unit

Lexile Levels 680L–790L

INTRODUCTION

Reading comprehension is the ability to understand and interpret text. To become confident and competent readers, students need to learn how to understand the literal meaning of a text and its vocabulary, and also its implied and inferred meaning.

This workbook is organised into four terms of work with 40 step-by-step lessons that focus on specific comprehension skills. To further support students, 8 grammar lessons target language usage. By looking carefully at words, clauses and sentences, students are better equipped to understand the texts they read. Each terms ends with a summative assessment that identifies students' strengths and rewards progress.

Step-by-step Comprehension

The 40 comprehension lessons teach key strategies for students to use when they read. Each lesson uses a levelled extract and focuses on a single comprehension strategy, with clear, easy-to-read instructions.

Students find key details in the text and highlight words and phrases. This ensures students have knowledge of the text before answering comprehension questions. The extracts are organised in a progressive sequence with clear modelling and built-in support. By focusing on a single strategy at a time, students develop their literal, inferential and critical comprehension skills, as well as extending their vocabulary.

Integrated Grammar

The eight grammar lessons in this book aim to help students understand how the English language system works, and how to apply this knowledge to texts.

Each lesson teaches a key concept in grammar. The focus is on connecting grammatical terms to text in meaningful ways. The instructional information box explains the concept and shows examples. Students then annotate a text and answer questions to identify the grammar in action. Questions increase in difficulty and include NAPLAN-style questions. The grammar lessons help students comprehend and connect with a broad range of texts.

The Reading Eggspress Online Lessons

Reading Eggspress provides a comprehensive and systematic online program that models, scaffolds and supports reading comprehension. The 220 lessons have been organised in a clear progression to develop reading comprehension skills for students in Years 1–6. Each lesson includes built-in motivational elements to reward efforts and boost students' enthusiasm for reading.

The workbook lessons can be completed as a stand-alone reading comprehension course, but when combined with the online lessons they act as a powerful boost to students' reading comprehension skills. Students using the online program show significant year-on-year improvements in both reading comprehension skills and higher reading levels, as highlighted in the program's detailed reporting module.

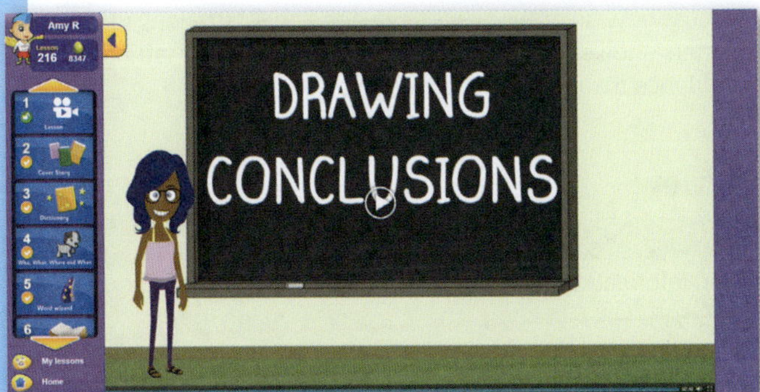

Engaging lessons

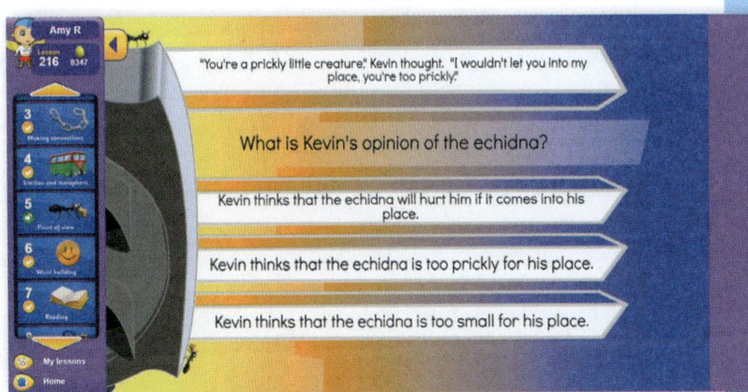

Interactive activities

The Library 4000+ ebooks

Students can practise their comprehension skills by reading ebooks in the Reading Eggspress Library. Search by topic, series, author, Lexile, reading age or book title to find the perfect book. With illustrated chapter books, full colour nonfiction books, poetry collections and a range of classics, there are texts to suit all readers and their capabilities.

New titles are added regularly with audio for all lower level books.

The Stadium

Compete in real time against students from around the country and around the world. These exciting head-to-head contests test skills in one of four areas—spelling, vocabulary, usage or grammar.

Reading Eggspress Workbooks and the Australian Curriculum

Each workbook lesson focuses on a core comprehension strategy or key concept in grammar. The texts, strategies and concepts were developed to align with the Australian Curriculum.

Year 3 Literacy

Analysing, interpreting and evaluating

AC9E3LY04 Read a range of texts using phonic, semantic and grammatical knowledge to read accurately and fluently, re-reading and self-correcting when required

AC9E3LY05 Use comprehension strategies when listening and viewing to build literal and inferred meaning, and begin to evaluate texts by drawing on a growing knowledge of context, text structures and language features

Year 3 Language

Text structure and organisation

AC9E3LA03 Describe how texts across the curriculum use different language features and structures relevant to their purpose

Language for expressing and developing ideas

AC9E3LA06 Understand that a clause is a unit of grammar usually containing a subject and a verb that need to agree

AC9E3LA08 Understand that verbs are anchored in time through tense

AC9E3LA10 Extend topic-specific and technical vocabulary and know that words can have different meanings in different contexts

AC9E3LA11 Understand that apostrophes signal missing letters in contractions, and apostrophes are used to show singular and plural possession

Year 3 Literature

Examining literature

AC9E3LE03 Discuss how an author uses language and illustrations to portray characters and settings in texts, and explore how the settings and events influence the mood of the narrative

Reading Eggspress Comprehension Strategy Overview

Comprehension	Strategy	Fiction Lessons	Nonfiction Lessons
Literal Looks for explicitly stated answers in the texts. Answers **Who**, **What**, **When** and **Where** questions.	Finding Facts and Information	61, 83	66, 86
	Main Idea and Details	73	79, 90, 97
	Think Marks	64	
	Sequencing Events	75, 82, 94	69, 98
Inferential Finds implied information in the text. Looks for **text clues** and evidence that point to the correct answer.	Cause and Effect	91	68, 80, 88
	Compare and Contrast		67, 76
	Drawing Conclusions	62	78
	Making Inferences	74, 92	99
	Making Predictions	65	
Critical Asks for **connections** or **opinions** on information in the text. Uses text clues to support the connections.	Analysing Character Actions	81	
	Making Connections	72, 85, 93	87
	Visualisation	71, 95	89
	Point of View	63, 84	77, 96, 100
Vocabulary Uses context clues and own knowledge to understand key words in the text.	Word Study		70

Reading Eggspress Grammar Overview

Grammar	Focus	Fiction Lessons	Nonfiction Lessons
Sentence Looks at how **clauses** are structured and how they come together to **build** cohesive sentences.	Subject/verb agreement		2
	Noun phrases		4
	Conjunctions	5	
	Adverbs of time		6
	Prepositional phrases		8
Text Assesses paragraph **composition** to see how sentences work together to create cohesive texts.	Continuous tense	3	
Punctuation Models correct punctuation **usage** for different types of words, clauses and sentences.	Direct Speech	1	

STUDENT RECORD SHEET

Use this page to record the number of questions you answered correctly for each lesson.

Term 1

Map 13 Fiction Lessons 560L–640L	61 Finding Facts and Information	62 Drawing Conclusions	63 Point of View	64 Think Marks	65 Making Predictions	Grammar 1 Direct Speech	
Map 14 Nonfiction Lessons 630L–710L	66 Finding Facts and Information	67 Compare and Contrast	68 Cause and Effect	69 Sequencing Events	70 Word Study	Grammar 2 Subject/Verb Agreement	Assessment 1 *The Tiger, the Man and the Jackal*

Term 2

Map 15 Fiction Lessons 620L–660L	71 Visualisation	72 Making Connections	73 Main Idea and Details	74 Making Inferences	75 Sequencing Events	Grammar 3 Continuous Tense	
Map 16 Nonfiction Lessons 680L–720L	76 Compare and Contrast	77 Point of View	78 Drawing Conclusions	79 Main Idea and Details	80 Cause and Effect	Grammar 4 Noun Phrases	Assessment 2 *The Great Wall of China*

Term 3

Map 17 Fiction Lessons 640L–700L	81 Analysing Character Actions	82 Sequencing Events	83 Finding Facts and Information	84 Point of View	85 Making Connections	Grammar 5 Conjunctions	
Map 18 Nonfiction Lessons 700L–740L	86 Finding Facts and Information	87 Making Connections	88 Cause and Effect	89 Visualisation	90 Main Idea and Details	Grammar 6 Adverbs of Time	Assessment 3 *Flight of the Falcon*

Term 4

Map 19 Fiction Lessons 690L–780L	91 Cause and Effect	92 Making Inferences	93 Making Connections	94 Sequencing Events	95 Visualisation	Grammar 7 Apostrophes and Contractions	
Map 20 Nonfiction Lessons 680L–790L	96 Point of View	97 Main Idea and Details	98 Sequencing Events	99 Making Inferences	100 Point of View	Grammar 8 Prepositional Phrases	Assessment 4 *The Emu*

LESSON 61

Shugg's Pet Octopus

Finding Facts and Information

To find facts and information in a text, we usually ask the questions **Who? What? Where?** or **When?** The answers can be clearly seen in the text.

Read the passage.

Highlight where Shugg and Katie were going.

Underline what Duke asked Shugg.

Circle how Duke got Shugg's backpack.

Colour where Duke threw Shugg's backpack.

Later, as Shugg and Katie walked home through the park, Duke stepped out from behind a tree. "Trying to scare me, were you?"

"No," said Shugg.

Duke snatched Shugg's backpack and threw it up into a very tall tree. He stood under the tree with his hands on his hips. "Now let's see you climb up and get it."

Circle the correct answer for each question.

1. **Where** were Shugg and Katie going?
   - a to school
   - b to the park
   - c home
   - d to the beach

2. **What** does Duke ask Shugg?
   - a May I look inside your backpack?
   - b May I look at your octopus?
   - c Where can we play this afternoon?
   - d Were you trying to scare me?

3. **How** did Duke get Shugg's backpack?
   - a He snatched it.
   - b He asked for it.
   - c He bought it.
   - d He tossed it.

4. **Who** threw Shugg's backpack?
   - a Duke
   - b Miss Stinger
   - c Katie
   - d Cal

5. **Where** did Shugg's backpack land?
   - a up a tree
   - b under a tree
   - c into the lake
   - d under a chair

AC9E3LY05 Use comprehension strategies to build literal meaning

Read the passage.

Highlight who saw the backpack.

Put a box around where the backpack was.

Circle when Shugg raided the pantry.

Peter looked down at the backpack poking out from under the bed. Then he shook his head. "Nah! Not even you would bring home an octopus."

Later that night, Shugg raided the pantry. He found a tin of crab meat and some lobster-flavoured noodles. He opened both and pushed them under the bed.

Colour Peter's words.

Underline the things that Shugg found in the pantry.

6 **Who** looked down at the backpack?

7 **Where** was the backpack?

8 **What** did Peter say?

9 **When** did Shugg raid the pantry?

10 **What** did Shugg find in the pantry?

LESSON 62

No Problem!

Drawing Conclusions

To draw conclusions from a text, we have to use clues to make our own judgements. The clues help us find the answers that are hiding in the text.

Read the passage.

Circle the word that tells us Jack was enjoying the movie.

Highlight the word that tells what Jack's room looked like.

Circle what the movie was about.

Put a box around the narrator's name.

Underline why Jack didn't want to turn off the television.

It was Sunday afternoon. I was in my bedroom watching a good movie about aliens when Mum poked her head in. You could tell by the look on her face that she wasn't happy.

"Just look at the state of this room, Jack," she said. "It looks like a pigsty. Turn off the television and clean it up."

"In a minute," I answered, wishing she'd go away. The aliens were about to attack Earth and I wanted to see what was going to happen.

Circle the correct answer for each question.

1. Which is the best **conclusion**? Jack was watching a ...
   - a comedy.
   - b cartoon.
   - c science fiction movie.
   - d horror movie.
2. Which word is the **clue** to question 1's answer?
   - a bedroom
   - b aliens
   - c good
   - d watching
3. Which is the best **conclusion**? Jack's room was ...
   - a muddy.
   - b spotless.
   - c organised.
   - d messy.
4. Which word is the **clue** to question 3's answer?
   - a pigsty
   - b state
   - c clean
   - d television
5. **Which phrase tells us** that the movie was at an exciting point?
   - a In a minute
   - b go away
   - c about to attack
   - d wanted to see

AC9E3LY05 Use comprehension strategies to build inferred meaning

Read the passage.

Put a box around who Jack asked where his lunch was.

Circle the word that suggests that Jack was in a bad mood.

I asked Mum where she'd put my lunch. Usually it was on the bench.

"Oh, I don't do lunches," Mum said. "You have to make your own sandwiches."

"I'm already late," I grumbled. "You're going to have to drive me to school."

Mum shook her head. "I don't think so, dear. I don't run a taxi service. You'll have to walk."

Grabbing my school bag, I raced out the door. Thanks to Mum, I didn't have a hope of getting to school on time.

On the way I tried to think of a good excuse to tell my teacher. I decided it was easier to tell Mr Jones the truth.

Colour the reason Jack wanted Mum to drive him to school.

Underline who Jack blamed for being late for school.

6 What can we **conclude** about who usually made Jack's lunch?

7 What is the **clue** to question 6's answer?

8 Why can we **conclude** that Jack had probably overslept?

9 **How do we know** that Jack was going to be late for school?

10 Why can we **conclude** that Jack thought it was his mum's fault that he was going to be late for school?

LESSON 63

Kalo Li's New Country

Point of View

To identify point of view, we have to look at the way characters act and feel. The clues are in the way they express their opinions (what they think and believe).

Read the passage.

Circle the food the narrator likes best.

Highlight why the narrator likes the old people.

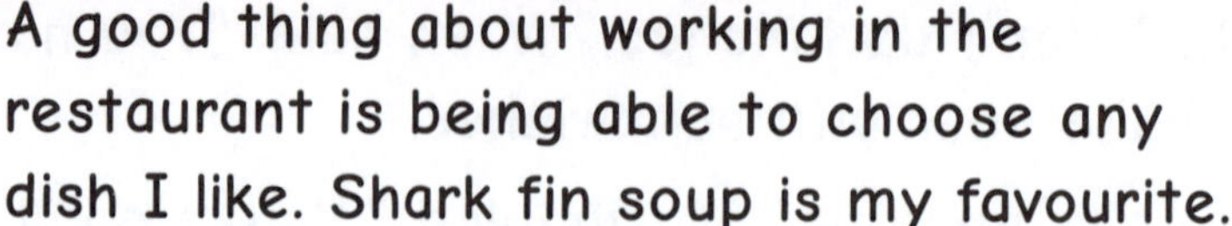

A good thing about working in the restaurant is being able to choose any dish I like. Shark fin soup is my favourite.

Some customers are funny and have a joke with you. Old people seem to be easier to talk to.

Others aren't so nice. When they order their food, they say things like, "No salt. No soy sauce. Be quick about it."

I'm very careful when taking down their order, so that I get it right.

Underline the words the narrator uses to describe the customers.

Put a box around the adjective the narrator uses to describe shark fin soup.

Circle the correct answer for each question.

1 From the narrator's **point of view**, which is the best dish in the restaurant?
- a shark curry
- b shark fin soup
- c shark steaks
- d shark kebabs

2 How does the narrator express her **opinion** about the dish she likes most? She says …
- a it is delicious.
- b it's amazing.
- c she loves it.
- d it's her favourite.

3 What is the narrator's **opinion** of the older customers? She …
- a thinks they are funny.
- b doesn't like them.
- c likes them.
- d is scared of them.

4 How does the narrator express her **opinion** of the older customers? She says they …
- a are easier to talk to.
- b tell funny jokes.
- c don't like salt.
- d are in a hurry.

5 What is the narrator's overall **opinion** of the customers?
- a She likes them all.
- b She doesn't like any of them.
- c Some are nice and others are not so nice.
- d She thinks they are rude.

AC9E3LY05 Use comprehension strategies to build inferred meaning

Read the passage.

Circle what the principal thinks of Hong Kong food.

Put a box around the pronouns that show that Kalo is the narrator.

Colour a sentence that shows that Kalo feels nervous.

Our school had a Food Day. Mum made me some honey king prawns to take to school.

The principal was very impressed with our Hong Kong food.

On Friday, the principal said, "We're going to visit your restaurant, Kalo. My staff and I will be coming tomorrow night for dinner."

My face went red. I wondered what the principal would order. What if he didn't like the food? What if I dropped a spring roll on him? What would my principal say to Mum? I was not the best student in the school.

Underline a sentence that makes you feel sympathy for Kalo.

Highlight what kind of a student Kalo thinks she is.

6 What was the principal's **opinion** of food from Hong Kong?

____

7 How do we know that the events in the story are told from Kalo's **point of view**?

____

____

8 How does Kalo **feel** about the principal and his staff coming to visit her restaurant?

____

____

9 Which sentence gives the best **clue** to question 8's answer?

____

10 What is Kalo's **opinion** of herself as a student?

____

LESSON 64

The Lazy Tortoise

Think Marks

To help us understand what we are reading, we can use special marks to identify the parts of a text we can see clearly, the parts we don't understand, and the personal connections we make to situations in the text.

Read the passage.

If you can see question 1's answer clearly place a ☺ next to it.

If you had to look up the meaning of the word *heron*, place a **W** next to it. If you knew the meaning, place a ✓ next to it.

All the animals of the world were very excited.

"The great god Jupiter is getting married, and we're all invited to the wedding!" said a heron.

"What about me?" asked a cockroach. "Are you sure that even the small creatures are invited?"

"Yes, every one of us," replied a skink. "Jupiter said that every living creature is invited to the wedding."

Soon, an amazing swarm of living creatures began to head to the palace!

If you had to look up the meaning of the word skink, place a **W** next to it. If you knew the meaning, place a ✓ next to it.

If you can see question 4's answer place a ☺ next to it.

Draw a chain next to a situation you can connect to.

Circle the correct answer for each question.

1. How were all the animals of the world **feeling**?
   - a happy
   - b excited
   - c confused
   - d sad
2. What kind of creature is a **heron**?
   - a a reptile
   - b a marsupial
   - c an insect
   - d a bird

3. What is a **skink**?
   - a a type of snake
   - b a type of bird
   - c a type of lizard
   - d a type of monkey
4. Where were all the creatures **going**?
   - a to the palace
   - b to the jungle
   - c to the zoo
   - d to the park
5. Which of the following situations can most of us **connect** to?
   - a going to a god's wedding
   - b walking with a swarm of animals
   - c talking to a cockroach
   - d feeling excited about something

Read the passage.

If you can see question 6's answer clearly place a ☺ next to it.

Place a ✓ next to question 7's answer to show that you understand that part of the text.

If you had to look up the meanings of snug and cosy, place a **W** next to the words. If you knew the answer, use a ✓ instead.

Only after the wedding, when all the guests were enjoying a feast, did the tortoise plod up to the palace. Jupiter was very cross.

"Why are you so late?" he demanded. "Every other creature in the world managed to be at my wedding, but not you."

"Well, I didn't want to leave my home," said the tortoise. "I was happy at home, all snug and cosy."

Jupiter was furious. The tortoise would rather be in his filthy ditch than in his royal palace!

"So it shall be!" he said. "If you love your home so much, you will carry it on your back for the rest of your life!"

Do you understand how Jupiter punished the tortoise? If you do, place a ✓ next to the answer.

Draw a chain next to the part of the text that you can connect to.

Place a ✓ next to furious if you know what it means. Use a **W** if you are unsure of its meaning.

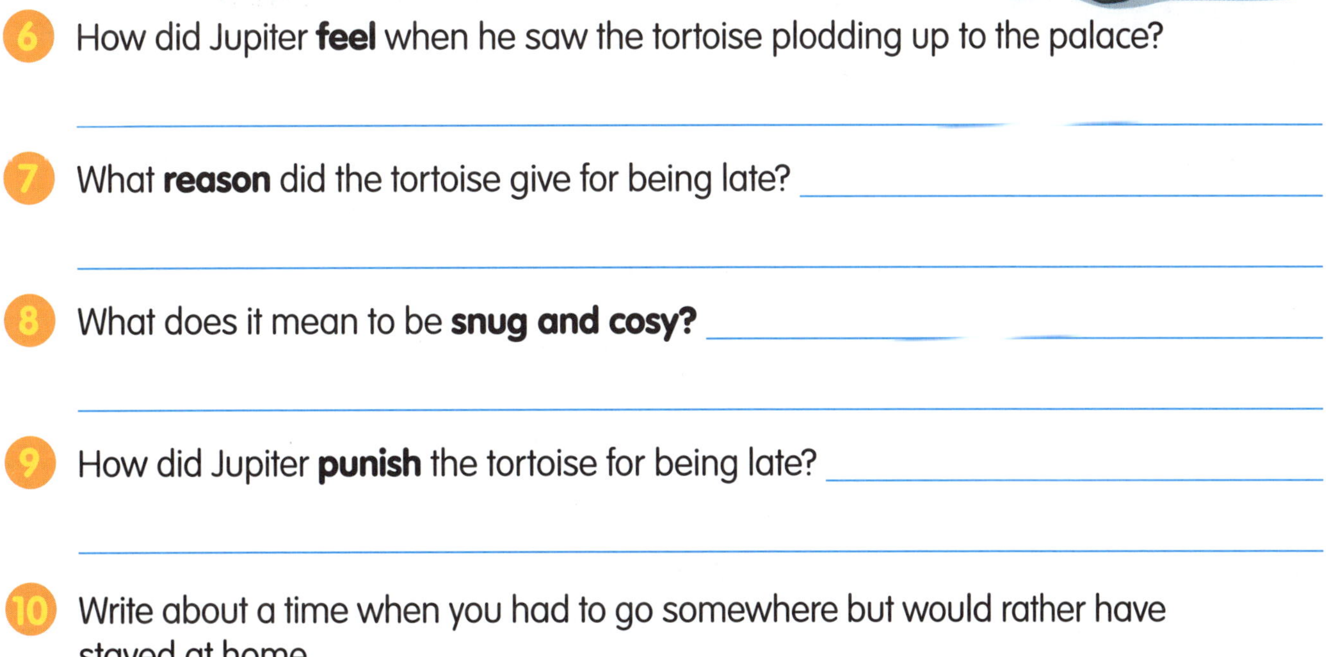

6 How did Jupiter **feel** when he saw the tortoise plodding up to the palace?

____

7 What **reason** did the tortoise give for being late? _______________

____

8 What does it mean to be **snug and cosy?** _______________

____

9 How did Jupiter **punish** the tortoise for being late? _______________

____

10 Write about a time when you had to go somewhere but would rather have stayed at home.

____

____

LESSON 65

What Kind of Pirate?

Making Predictions

We can predict what is going to happen in a text based on clues in the words and pictures and what we already know.

Read the passage.

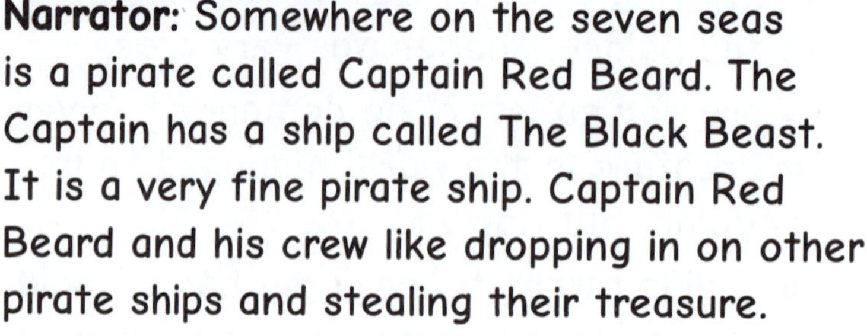

Circle a word that tells us what Captain Red Beard and his crew like to collect.

Put a box around the word that shows how Captain Red Beard and his crew get their treasure.

Narrator: Somewhere on the seven seas is a pirate called Captain Red Beard. The Captain has a ship called The Black Beast. It is a very fine pirate ship. Captain Red Beard and his crew like dropping in on other pirate ships and stealing their treasure.

Fingers: Pirate ship on the starboard bow, Captain.

Captain Red Beard: Good spotting, Fingers. Happy seadogs! Let's meet them.

Ahoy there fellow pirates! Can my crew and I board your ship? We could swap a few pirate tales of terror and treasure.

Underline the things Captain Red Beard and his crew like to do.

Highlight the question Captain Red Beard asks.

Colour the reason Captain Red Beard gives for wanting to board the ship.

Circle the correct answers for each question.

1. What two **predictions** can you make about what will happen next in the story?
   - a Captain Red Beard and his crew will invite the other crew onto their ship.
   - b Captain Red Beard and his crew will board the pirate ship.
   - c Captain Red Beard and his crew will shout louder.
   - d Captain Red Beard and his crew will steal the pirates' treasure.
   - e Captain Red Beard and his crew will tell the other pirates a story.

2. What **evidence** is there in the text to support your predictions? Choose three answers.
   - a Captain Red Beard and his crew like dropping in on other pirate ships.
   - b Captain Red Beard's ship is called The Black Beast.
   - c Captain Red Beard and his crew like stealing other pirates' treasure.
   - d Fingers spotted a ship on the starboard bow.
   - e Captain Red Beard wants to meet the pirates on the other ship.

Read the passage.

Underline the adjectives Captain Red Beard uses to describe Captain Rat's crew.

Narrator: Captain Red Beard had an idea.

Captain Red Beard: Nasty? Yes, you are the nastiest pirates I have ever met. We would like to help you be nasty. You must decide on the nastiest thing you can do to us. My crew will go below decks while you have a nasty little meeting about it.

Narrator: Captain Rat thought this was a wonderfully nasty idea. His crew all argued about what was nastiest. Captain Red Beard and his crew went below.

Colour two sentences that help you understand what Captain Red Beard and his crew are planning to do.

3 What **prediction** can you make about what Captain Red Beard is planning to do?

____

____

4 What do you know about pirates that **helped you** make your prediction?

____

____

5 What **prediction** can you make about what Captain Rat and his crew are going to do to Captain Red Beard and his crew?

____

____

6 What **evidence** is there in the text that helped you make your prediction?

____

____

AC9E3LY05 Use comprehension strategies to make predictions in a text

GRAMMAR LESSON 1

Direct Speech

Direct speech repeats the exact words someone says. **Quotation marks** or **speech marks** (" ") are placed around the speaker's words, **including any punctuation**. For example:

"Which is your favourite?" asked Olivia.

Ben said, "I like chocolate ice cream."

The **first word** a person says always starts with a **capital letter**, even if it comes after a comma.

Read the extract.

Circle all of the speech marks in the passage.

In this sentence, underline the punctuation that comes after the last word Dad speaks.

In these sentences, **highlight** the punctuation that comes after the last word Oliver speaks.

A Country is Born

The caravan in my backyard is the best place to hang out after school. I have all I need in here—a bed, a microwave, even a television.

Knock, knock! I open the caravan door.

"I want to see your school report, Oliver," says Dad, standing on the step. I've been waiting for this. Dad told me weeks ago I must get a good report.

"I've got the best report in the whole school—maybe even Australia," I boast, giving it to him.

"Wow, this is great," he says.

"I know. Suzie is one of the smartest kids in the state!"

"Good for her. But I want your report, written about you," he says.

Circle the correct answer for each question.

In the following sentences, which punctuation is missing?

1. "I want to see your school report, Oliver" says Dad.

   a . b , c . d !

2. "I've got the best report in the whole school—maybe even Australia, I boast.

   a " b ! c . d "

3. Wow, this is great," he says.

   a " b . c ? d "

4. "I know. Suzie is one of the smartest kids in the state"

   a , b ? c ! d "

5. "Good for her. But I want your report, written about you" he says.

   a . b , c ? d "

AC9E3LA03 Describe how texts use structures relevant to their purpose

6 **In the following sentences, fill in the speech marks.**

- **a** Oliver has photocopied my school report, said Suzie.
- **b** Oliver said, I wish my school report was as good as Suzie's.
- **c** When are you going to do your homework? asked Dad.
- **d** What a brilliant project this is! exclaimed my teacher.
- **e** James said, Have your parents seen your report yet?

7 **Which sentence has the correct punctuation? Tick.**

- **a** ☐ "Maths is my favourite subject", said Joshua.
- **b** ☐ "Have you learnt for the test? asked Maria.
- **c** ☐ The teacher said, "the children are in the library."
- **d** ☐ "Put your lunch in your school bag," said Mum.

8 **In the following sentences, choose the correct option to fill each gap.**

a "Do you know the answer to this ________ asked Mr Jones.

○ question"? ○ question?" ○ question," ○ question."

b "Help me carry the sports equipment to the ________ said Miss Liu.

○ field." ○ field," ○ field", ○ field"?

9 **Use the information in the speech bubbles to complete the sentences. Don't forget the quotation marks!**

Oliver asked, ______________________________

____

____

Suzy replied, ______________________________

____

LESSON 66

Trees

Finding Facts and Information

To find facts and information in a text, we usually ask the questions **Who? What? Where?** or **When?** The answers can be clearly seen in the text.

Read the passage.

Colour what big, flat leaves can do.

Put a box around when some deciduous trees lose their leaves.

Highlight four words that describe the size of the leaves.

Most species of tree are broadleaf trees. They often have flat, wide leaves.

Big, flat leaves can catch lots of sunlight, and they need lots of water. Some broadleaf trees are deciduous and lose their leaves in winter.

Broadleaf evergreen trees, such as holly and orange trees, grow in warmer areas. They do not lose their leaves. Broadleaf evergreen trees have thicker, waxy leaves that often contain oil. The leaves can be large, small, long or short.

Broadleaf trees are flowering plants. New seeds grow from the flowers.

Underline where holly and orange trees grow.

Circle what is often found in broadleaf evergreen trees.

Highlight where new seeds come from.

Circle the correct answer for each question.

1. **What** are the big, flat leaves of broadleaf trees able to do? Catch lots of …
   a rainwater　b insects　c seeds　d sunlight
2. **When** do deciduous trees lose their leaves?
   a in summer　b in winter　c in autumn　d in spring
3. **Where** do holly and orange trees grow?
   a in warmer areas　b in cooler areas
   c in very hot areas　d in very cold areas
4. **What** do the leaves of broadleaf evergreen trees often contain?
   a fruits　b seeds　c oil　d roots
5. **Where** do the new seeds of broadleaf trees come from?
   a the stems　b the leaves　c the flowers　d the roots

AC9E3LY05 Use comprehension strategies to build literal meaning

Read the passage.

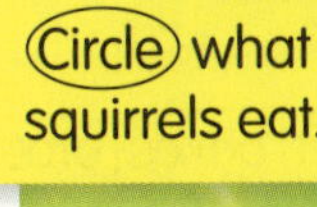

Circle what squirrels eat.

Underline where koalas live.

Highlight where birds build their nests.

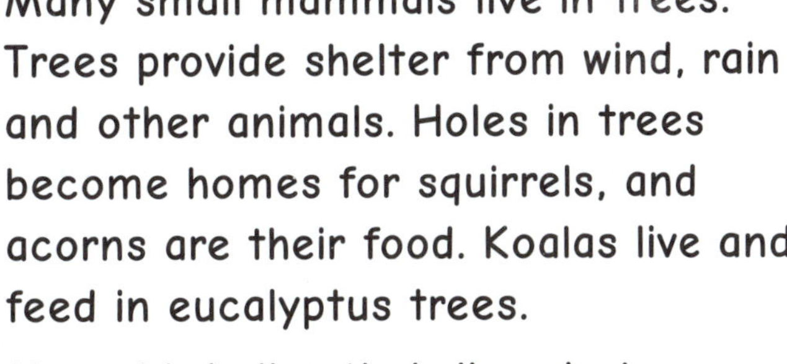

Many small mammals live in trees. Trees provide shelter from wind, rain and other animals. Holes in trees become homes for squirrels, and acorns are their food. Koalas live and feed in eucalyptus trees.

Many birds live their lives in trees. They build their nests in the branches or hollows of trees. Trees provide fruits, nectar and seeds for birds to eat.

Millions of insects live in trees. Many types of beetles, ants and butterflies depend on trees for food and shelter.

Colour three things that trees protect small mammals from.

Put a box around the things birds eat.

Underline examples of insects that depend on trees for food and shelter.

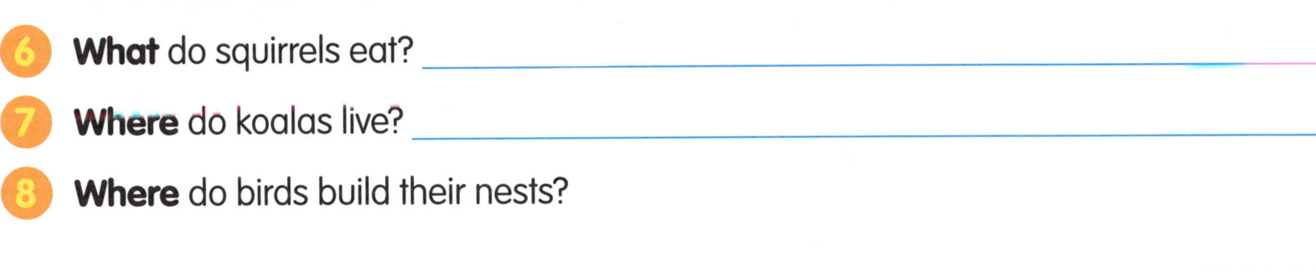

6 **What** do squirrels eat? ______________________

7 **Where** do koalas live? ______________________

8 **Where** do birds build their nests?

____

____

9 **What** do birds find to eat in trees?

____

____

10 **What** types of insects depend on trees for food and shelter?

____

____

LESSON 67

Plants as Food

Compare and Contrast

When we compare and contrast information, we look for the similarities and differences between details in the text.

Read the passage.

Highlight the words *peaches* and *cherries*. **Colour** the key words that tell us how they are similar.

Circle the words that tell about the kind of weather raspberries and apples prefer.

Stone fruits, fruits with pits, also grow on trees. They have one hard seed covered with soft flesh. Peaches, plums, cherries and apricots are stone fruits.

Many fruits are quite small. Strawberries, raspberries and blackberries are all small fruits with lots of seeds. They grow on small plants or bushes in cool areas.

Apples and pears grow on trees in cool areas. They both have a core with small seeds inside. Some apples are grown to make juice to drink.

Put boxes around the information about the seeds in peaches and in pears.

Underline the words that tell what kind of plants strawberries and blackberries grow on.

Carefully read the following sentences. Put a T next to the statements that are true, and an F next to the statements that are false.

1. ☐ Peaches and pears have the same number of seeds.
2. ☐ Peaches and pears grow on trees.
3. ☐ Cherries and strawberries are fruits.
4. ☐ Cherries and strawberries are both stone fruits.
5. ☐ Raspberries and apples prefer cooler weather.
6. ☐ Raspberries and apples are both small fruits.
7. ☐ Strawberries and blackberries grow on small plants or bushes.

AC9E3LY05 Use comprehension strategies to build inferred meaning

Read the passage.

Circle the key word that shows how honey and sugar are similar.

Underline what herbs and spices are used for.

Colour the words that tell how chocolate and vanilla are similar.

Many animals have a "sweet tooth". Birds and bees drink sweet nectar from flowers, and bears eat honey. People eat sugar made from the dried juice of sugar cane.

Herbs and spices are used in cooking. Herbs such as basil and parsley are used as seasoning. Garlic adds flavour, and chillies are hot and spicy.

Chocolate, vanilla and cinnamon are also plant flavours. Chocolate is made from seeds. Vanilla is made from seed pods, and cinnamon is ground from the dried bark of a tree.

Many drinks are made using plants. Coffee beans and tea leaves both come from plants. Lemonade is made from the juice of lemons.

Put a box around the sentence that shows how garlic and chillies are different.

Highlight the difference between chocolate and vanilla.

Circle two ways in which tea and coffee are similar.

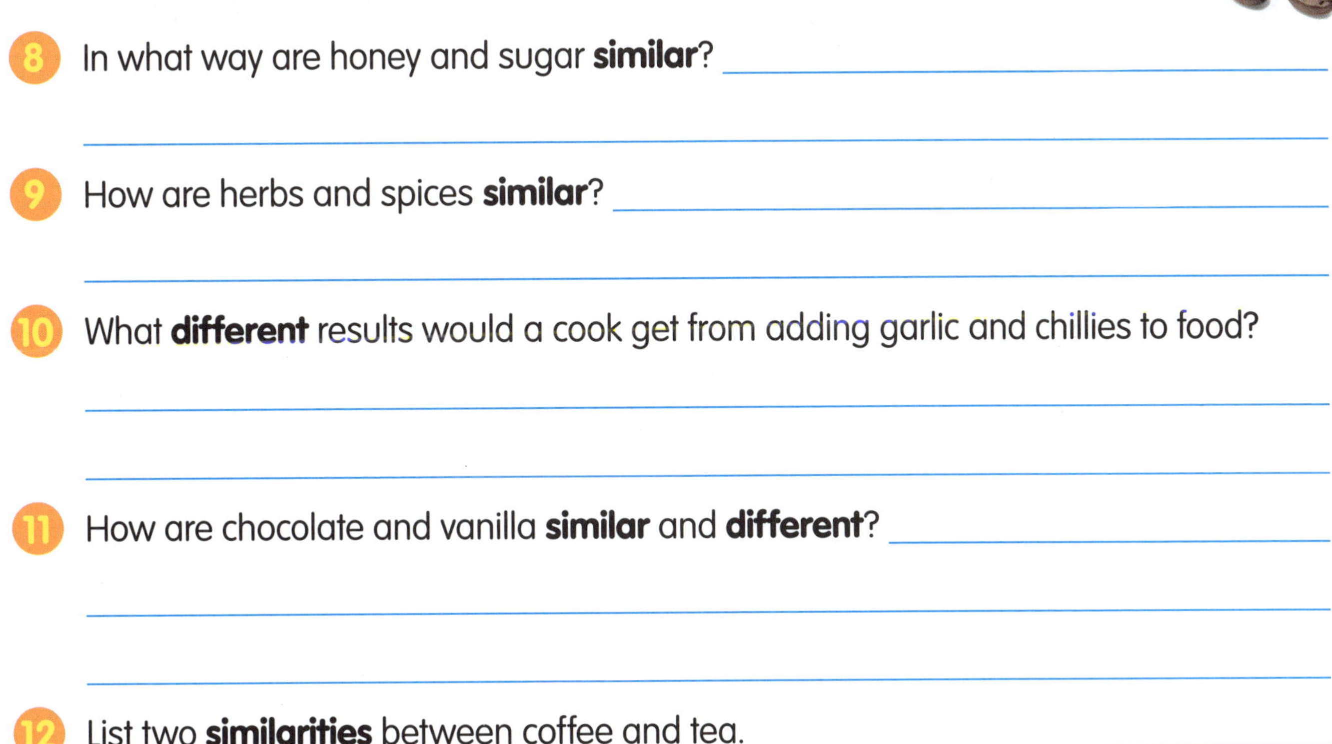

8 In what way are honey and sugar **similar**? ______

9 How are herbs and spices **similar**? ______

10 What **different** results would a cook get from adding garlic and chillies to food? ______

11 How are chocolate and vanilla **similar** and **different**? ______

12 List two **similarities** between coffee and tea. ______

LESSON 68

Grasslands

Cause and Effect

To find cause and effect, we ask why something happens and what the result is.

Read the passage.

Underline what forms when too little rain falls.

Colour what forms when lots of rain falls.

Put a box around the amount of rainfall grasslands need each year.

Grasslands are environments in which grass is the main plant, rather than shrubs or trees.

Grasslands need 25 to 100 centimetres of rain each year. If they get less than this, they turn into deserts. If grasslands get much more rain, lots of trees grow and they become forests.

There are two main types of grassland — savannas (also called tropical grasslands) and temperate grasslands.

Circle the correct answer for each question.

1. What **causes** deserts to form?
   - a hot weather
   - b fires
   - c not enough rain
   - d too much rain
2. What is the **effect** on the environment when too little rain falls?
   - a It turns into tropical grasslands.
   - b It turns into forests.
   - c It turns into temperate grasslands.
   - d It turns into deserts.
3. What **causes** forests to form?
   - a a high rainfall
   - b a low rainfall
   - c snow and ice
   - d flooding rivers
4. What is the **effect** on the environment when it rains a lot?
   - a Deserts form.
   - b Forests form.
   - c Mountains form.
   - d Rivers form.
5. What type of environment do we get when an area receives between 25 to 100 centimetres of rain a year?
   - a deserts
   - b forests
   - c grasslands
   - d tundras

AC9E3LY05 Use comprehension strategies to build inferred meaning

Read the passage.

Circle the cause of the grasses dying off.

Colour the effect the hot winds have on the grasses.

Underline why many animals migrate in the dry season.

Put a box around what happens when the waterholes dry up.

Highlight the reason the grasses don't completely die off.

Colour the reason the grasses start growing again.

The African savanna has cycles of dry and wet seasons.

1 Dry season

Hot winds begin to blow. Grasses die off at the surface, but the roots remain alive. Fires may burn whole areas. Waterholes dry up, causing many animals to migrate. There are often violent thunderstorms before the wet season starts.

2 Wet season

When the rain starts, grass can grow 2.5 centimetres in one day.

6 What **causes** grasses on the African savanna to die off?

____

7 What **effect** do hot winds have on the African savanna?

____

8 **Why** do many animals migrate in the dry season?

____

9 **What happens** when the waterholes dry up?

____

10 What **causes** the grass to start growing again?

____

Recipe Anzac Biscuits

Sequencing Events

To identify the sequence of events in a text, look at numbers and words that give clues to the order in which things happen.

Read the passage.

Underline what the recipe says to do first.

Circle the time words in Step 3.

Highlight what should be added after the rolled oats.

Put a box around what should be done after melting the butter and syrup.

Underline the final step.

Method

1. Turn on the oven to 180° Celsius. Put baking paper on the baking trays.
2. Place flour, sugar, rolled oats and coconut in the bowl.
3. Melt the butter and golden syrup in the small saucepan, and then add bicarbonate of soda and water.
4. Stir the wet mixture into the dry ingredients and mix well.

Circle the correct answer for each question.

1. What does the recipe tell you to do **first**?
   a put flour in the bowl b turn on the oven c add the water d melt the butter
2. What should you do **before** you add flour to the bowl?
   a put baking paper on the trays b add bicarbonate of soda and water
   c add the coconut d melt the butter and syrup
3. Which of the following ingredients is added **last** in Step 2?
   a rolled oats b flour c coconut d sugar
4. What should you do **after** you have melted the butter and syrup?
   a put paper on the trays b add the coconut
   c combine the wet and dry ingredients d add the bicarbonate of soda and water
5. Which is the **fourth step** in the recipe?
   a melting the butter and golden syrup b turning on the oven
   c adding coconut to the mixture d combining the wet and dry ingredients

AC9E3LY05 Use comprehension strategies to build literal and inferred meaning

Read the passage.

Underline where the small balls should be placed.

Highlight what should happen while the biscuits are baking.

5. Roll teaspoonfuls of mixture into small balls and place on the trays. Leave about 3 centimetres between them.
6. Bake for 10 to 15 minutes. Check the biscuits frequently to make sure they are not burning.
7. Let the biscuits cool slightly before lifting them off with a spatula, to cool on the wire rack.

Put a box around the amount of time the biscuits should spend in the oven.

Colour the key words that tell when to lift the biscuits off the tray.

Circle where the biscuits should cool.

6 What should you do **after** you roll the mixture into balls?

7 What should you do **after** placing the balls on the trays?

8 What should you do **while** the biscuits are baking?

9 **When** should you lift the biscuits off the tray?

10 What is the **final** thing you should do before you can eat the biscuits?

LESSON 70

Hoaxes, Fibs and Fakes

Word Study

We can often use clues in the text to help us work out the meaning of words we do not understand.

Read the passage.

Circle the word that tells us where the farmers got the spaghetti from.

Underline how many people did not know where spaghetti came from in the 1950's.

On April Fools' Day in 1957, an English TV program showed Swiss farmers picking spaghetti from trees. Hundreds of people called the TV station and asked how to grow spaghetti trees. They were told to "place a **sprig** of spaghetti in a tin of tomato sauce and hope for the best".

Because spaghetti was an **exotic** food in England at that time, many people didn't know where it came from. They believed that it could grow on trees!

Colour the word that tells us what nationality the farmers were.

Highlight the sentence that tells us why many English people believed the April Fools' joke.

Circle the correct answer for each question.

1. Some people in England wanted to grow their own spaghetti trees. A tree is a type of …
   - a animal.
   - b plant.
   - c rock.
   - d soil.
2. Based on question 1's answer, we can infer that the word **sprig** most likely means …
   - a tail.
   - b string.
   - c stem.
   - d ribbon.
3. In the 1950's, how many people in England did not know where spaghetti came from?
   - a very few
   - b one or two
   - c everyone
   - d many
4. In the TV program, who was picking spaghetti from the trees?
   - a English farmers
   - b local farmers
   - c Swiss farmers
   - d children
5. Based on question 3 and 4's answers, we can infer that the word **exotic** most likely means …
   - a from a foreign country.
   - b from the same country.
   - c from the earth.
   - d from a factory.

AC9E3LA10 Extend topic-specific and technical vocabulary and know that words can have different meanings in different contexts

Read the passage.

(Circle) three words that can help us work out what an astronomer does.

Underline words that can help us work out what gravity is.

We often believe things we read, especially things that sound scientific. On 1 April 1976, **astronomer** Patrick Moore announced that Pluto would pass behind Jupiter. He said that this would lessen the **gravity** on Earth. If people jumped in the air at the exact moment the planets were in line, they would be able to float — just like astronauts in space. Some people said they had floated up to the ceiling!

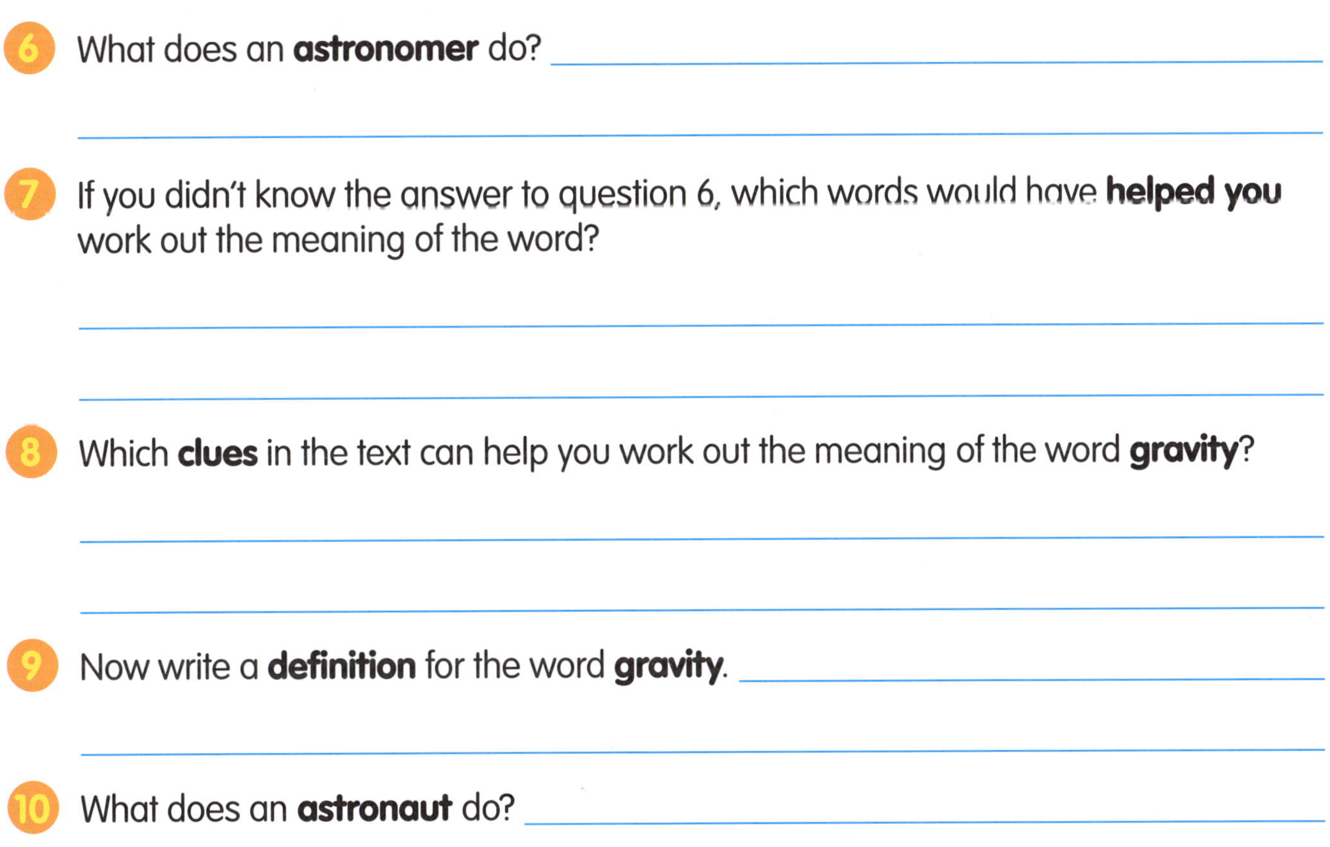

6. What does an **astronomer** do? ______________________________

____

7. If you didn't know the answer to question 6, which words would have **helped you** work out the meaning of the word?

____

____

8. Which **clues** in the text can help you work out the meaning of the word **gravity**?

____

____

9. Now write a **definition** for the word **gravity**. ______________________________

____

10. What does an **astronaut** do? ______________________________

____

GRAMMAR LESSON 2

Subject/Verb Agreement

In a sentence, the **subject** and the **verb** must agree with each other. For example: ***The boy*** (singular) ***kicks*** *the ball.* ***The boys*** (plural) ***kick*** *the ball.* ***The baby*** (singular) ***is*** *very cute.* ***The babies*** (plural) ***are*** *very cute.* ***The cat*** (singular) ***has*** *a bushy tail.* ***The cats*** (plural) ***have*** *bushy tails.*

Read the extract.

In this sentence, circle the subject and put a box around the verb.

In this sentence, **highlight** the subject and **colour** the verb.

In this sentence, underline the subject and circle the verb.

In this sentence, put a box around the subject and **highlight** the verb.

Crabs

Most crabs live in the sea. They have a hard, outer shell. The shell protects their soft body.

Crabs have five pairs of legs. The first two legs are claws. The claws are very useful. They hold and carry food. They dig into sand and mud. They crack open shells. They even scare off enemies.

Life in the wild is dangerous for crabs. Many animals prey on them.

Crabs use wonderful tricks to hide themselves. Some hide under rocks and in holes. Others bury themselves in the sand, or are the same colour as their surroundings.

Some crabs dress up to hide themselves. The seaweed decorator crab covers itself with seaweed. It snips off a piece of seaweed with its claws. Then it sticks the seaweed onto its shell. The crab has special hairs on its back. These hairs act like Velcro. They hold the decorations onto the crab's back.

In the following sentences, circle the subject.

1. They have a hard, outer shell.
   a hard b shell c They d have

2. Many animals prey on them.
   a Many b animals c Many animals d prey

3. It snips off a piece of seaweed with its claws.
   a piece b seaweed c claws d It

In the following sentences, circle the verb.

4. Then it sticks the seaweed onto its shell.
   a it b the c sticks d onto

5. The first two legs are claws.
   a are b first c two d legs

AC9E3LA06 Understand that a clause is a unit of grammar usually containing a subject and a verb that need to agree

6 Circle the verb that correctly completes each sentence.

a	Some crabs ________ on land.	**live**	**lives**
b	A crab _______ a crustacean.	**is**	**are**
c	A young crab ________ from an egg.	**hatch**	**hatches**
d	The hermit crab ________ no shell of its own.	**have**	**has**
e	Most hermit crabs _______ scavengers.	**is**	**are**
f	Sharks ________ a sharp sense of smell.	**have**	**has**

7 Choose the correct word or words to fill the gap.

a ____________ lay a large number of eggs.

○ A female crab ○ Female crabs ○ This female crab ○ An adult crab

b ____________ sheds its skin many times.

○ Young crabs ○ The young crabs ○ The young crab ○ Many young crabs

c ____________ make their nests on land.

○ A green turtle ○ The green turtle ○ This green turtle ○ Green turtles

8 Each sentence has one word that is incorrect. Circle it, and write the correction in the space.

a Hermit crabs eats rotting plants or dead animals. ____________

b The red hermit crab have hairy red legs. ____________

c Land crabs is active during the night. ____________

d A soldier crab walk forwards, not sideways. ____________

e Soldier crabs has round, blue bodies. ____________

f The whale shark are a very big fish. ____________

g Sharks feeds on seals and smaller fish. ____________

ASSESSMENT 1:

The Tiger, the Man and the Jackal

Lexile: 570L

A tiger once got caught in a cage. He asked a man passing by to free him. At first the man refused, worried the tiger would devour him. The tiger promised that he would do no such thing. The man felt sorry for the tiger and set him free. Immediately the tiger pounced on the man.

"What a fool you are!" said the tiger. "You will make a fine meal!"

The man pleaded for his life, reminding the tiger of his promise.

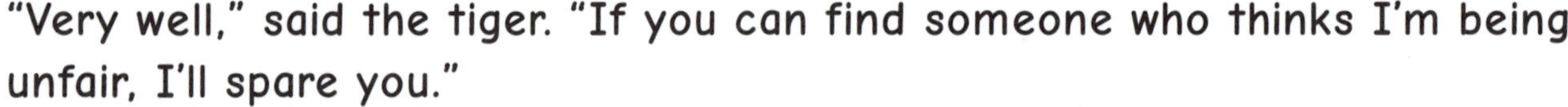

"Very well," said the tiger. "If you can find someone who thinks I'm being unfair, I'll spare you."

The man told his story to a tree, a road and a water buffalo. Not one of them thought the tiger was being unfair.

The man was beginning to give up hope when he met a jackal. The man told the jackal his story.

"I don't understand," said the jackal. "I need to see where this happened."

The man took the jackal to the place where the tiger waited. The savage creature was sharpening his claws, eager to start his meal. The tiger agreed that the man could tell his story one more time.

The jackal pretended that he didn't understand a word the man was saying. Eventually the tiger lost his patience.

"Look here, you silly jackal! This is how it happened! I was in the cage ..." explained the tiger as he stepped inside the cage.

Immediately the crafty jackal closed the door. Once again the tiger was trapped, but this time, the man knew better than to free him.

Circle the correct answer for each question.

1 Why did the man free the tiger? LITERAL
- a The tiger promised to reward the man.
- b The man felt sorry for the tiger.
- c The tiger was badly injured.
- d The man was not afraid of tigers.

2 What happened when the man freed the tiger? The tiger … LITERAL
- a ran away.
- b asked the man to follow him.
- c shut the man in the cage.
- d jumped on the man.

3 Which words best describe the man? INFERENTIAL
- a kind and trusting
- b kind and proud
- c kind and clever
- d kind and brave

4 Who did the man speak to first? LITERAL
- a the water buffalo
- b the jackal
- c the road
- d the tree

5 What was the tiger's opinion of the man? The tiger thought the man was … INFERENTIAL
- a brave.
- b clumsy.
- c foolish.
- d kind.

6 Which word best describes the tiger? INFERENTIAL
- a untrustworthy
- b trustworthy
- c fair
- d patient

7 What is the most likely reason that the tree, the road and the water buffalo agreed that the tiger was not being unfair? CRITICAL
- a Tigers naturally prey on other mammals.
- b They were scared of the tiger.
- c They did not like the man.
- d The tiger was their friend.

8 Where was the tiger waiting for the man? LITERAL
- a next to the tree
- b on the road
- c at the man's house
- d by the cage

9 How did the jackal help the man? CRITICAL
- a by defeating the tiger in a fight
- b by frightening the tiger
- c by chasing the tiger away
- d by tricking the tiger

10 What is the main message of this story? LITERAL
- a Do not trust a jackal.
- b Kindness is not always rewarded.
- c Tigers are savage animals.
- d Stay away from cages.

LESSON 71

Cinquains

Visualisation

Visualising the people, places, things and events we are reading about helps build better understanding of the text. Looking for key words in the text will help us create images that match the text.

Read the poems.

In Poem 1, circle the words that helped you see what was happening in the tree.

1. Tree
Giant, strong
Climbing, swinging, playing
Fun among the branches
Gum

3. Spider
Hairy, hidden
Seeing, watching, knowing
Waits with all patience
Strikes

In Poem 2, **colour** the words that helped you see what the spaghetti looked like on the fork.

2. Spaghetti
Loopy, meaty
Slurping, slipping, twisting
Between my fork and mouth
Yum

In Poem 3, underline the words that helped you see what the spider was doing.

Read each of the poems again. As you do so, visualise what you are reading about. Draw a picture of the images from each poem.

Poem 1

Poem 3

Poem 2

AC9E3LE03 Discuss how an author uses language and illustrations to portray characters and settings in texts, and explore how the settings and events influence the mood of the narrative

Read the poems.

Circle the words that tell you what the zebra looked like.

Highlight the words that helped you see why the zebra ran.

1. Zebra
Black and white stripes
Grazing on shrubs and leaves
Sudden snorts, the smell of lion
Run!

Underline the words that tell you where the balloons were.

Put a box around the words that helped you see what the children were doing.

2. Balloons
Pink, white and blue
Bobbing in the garden
Happy children eating, playing
Party!

Colour the words that helped you see how the shoes moved.

Circle the words that helped you visualise how the person wearing the shoes felt.

3. New shoes
Shiny, squeaky
Stepping, striding, stomping
Hurting my heels, pinching my toes
Ouch!

Read each of the poems again. As you do so, visualise what you are reading about. Draw a picture of the images as you read each poem.

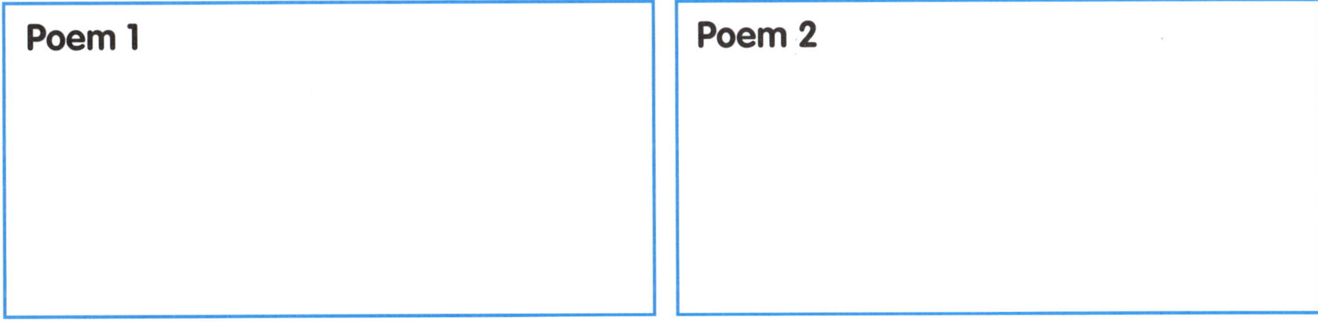

Poem 3

AC9E3LE03 Discuss how an author uses language and illustrations to portray characters and settings in texts, and explore how the settings and events influence the mood of the narrative

LESSON 72

The Fine Line

Making Connections

When you read a text, it is important to keep track of all the characters. You need to see the link between the nouns and pronouns so that you know who the pronouns are referring to.

Read the passage.

Circle the pronoun "I" and the noun it refers to.

Underline the pronoun that stands in place of "Garth and Snake".

Put a box around the pronoun "she" and the person it refers to.

"Where are you going, Garth?" Mum called as I tried to slip out the front door.

I tried to tell myself it was only half a lie. I was going to Snake's place, I just wasn't staying there.

We sat out the front of his place while I put on my blades.

"Garth, if my mum asks," he said, standing up, "just say we went to the park, okay?" He laughed. "What she doesn't know won't hurt her, right? Come on."

Highlight the pronoun "myself" and the noun it refers to.

Circle the correct answer for each question.

1. In the text, who does the **pronoun** "I" refer to?
   a Snake b Snake's mum c Garth's mum d Garth

2. In paragraph 3, which **noun** could replace the pronoun "his"?
   a Garth's b Snake's c Snake d Garth

3. In paragraph 4, who is speaking?
   a Snake b Garth c Snake's mum d Garth's mum

4. In paragraph 4, who does the **pronoun** "we" refer to? Snake and …
   a his brother b his mum c Garth d his dad

5. In paragraph 4, which phrase could replace the **pronoun** "she"?
   a your mum b my mum c his mum d their mum

AC9E3LA03 Describe how texts use different language features and structures

Read the passage.

Circle narrator's name.

Underline the pronoun "We" and the nouns it refers to.

Colour two pronouns that stand in place of the words "the dog".

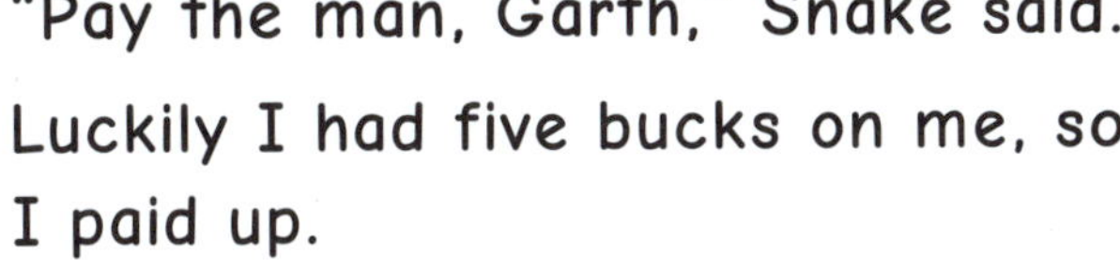

"Pay the man, Garth," Snake said.

Luckily I had five bucks on me, so I paid up.

We sat outside in the gutter to eat. We chose a spot so we could watch some builders working nearby.

One of the builders had a dog. He sniffed at us. I offered him a chip.

He liked that and he was coming back for another chip when Snake finished the last of his drink. He threw the can at him.

Highlight two different pronouns that stand in place of the phrase "Garth and Snake".

6 Who does the **pronoun** "I" refer to?

7 Which **nouns** could replace the **pronoun** "we"?

8 Who sniffed at us?

9 Who did Snake throw the can at?

10 In the last sentence, who do the **pronouns** "He" and "him" refer to?

LESSON 73

The North Wind and the Sun

Finding the Main Idea and Supporting Details

The main idea of a text is its key point. It sums up what the text is about. Details in the text can help us identify the main idea.

Read the passage.

Underline the sentence that best expresses the main idea of the text.

Highlight the sentence that supports the main idea.

Put a box around a sentence that shows what effect the Wind had on the man.

The Wind and the Sun had a competition to see who could make the man take off his coat. The Wind began to blow as hard as he could. He blew directly on the man with a whipping, punching wind. The man became cold and wrapped his coat closely around his body. No matter how hard the Wind blew, it was useless—the man only held his coat more tightly.

Circle the correct answer/s for each question.

1. Which sentence best expresses the **main idea** of the text?
   - a The Wind tried hard to frighten the man.
   - b The Wind tried hard to make the man take off his coat.
   - c The Wind tried hard to make the man hold on to his coat.
   - d The Wind tried hard to make the man cold.

2. Which **three details** support the main idea?
   - a The Wind whipped and punched around the man.
   - b The man became cold.
   - c The Wind blew directly on the man.
   - d The man wrapped his coat closely around his body.
   - e The man held his coat more tightly.
   - f The Wind blew as hard as he could.

AC9E3LY05 Use comprehension strategies to build literal and inferred meaning

Read the passage.

Highlight the Sun's actions.

Underline the words that show what the Sun made the man do. This will help you find the answer to question 3.

Now it was the Sun's turn. She came out from behind the cloud and shone brightly. The man began to sweat from the heat and decided he could go no further. So he stopped, took off his coat and continued his walk.

Put a box around a sentence that shows what effect the Sun had on the man.

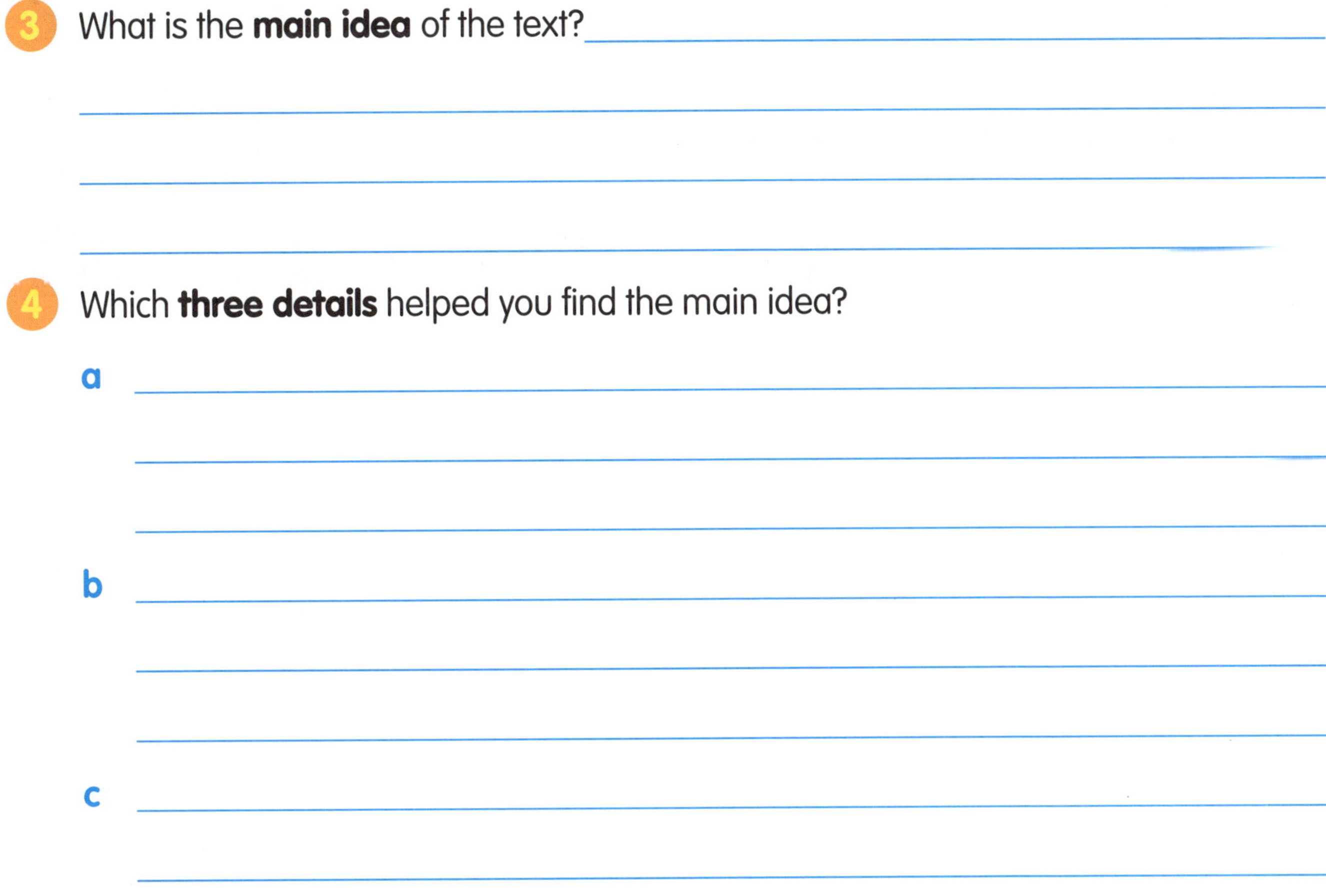

3 What is the **main idea** of the text? ______________________

____

____

____

4 Which **three details** helped you find the main idea?

a ______________________

____

____

b ______________________

____

____

c ______________________

____

____

LESSON 74

Invisi-pets

Making Inferences

To make inferences while reading, we have to use clues in the text. The clues help us find the answers that are hiding in the text.

Read the passage.

Circle the words that tell us what colour Wuzzy was.

Underline the sentence that gives the best description of Wuzzy.

Highlight the words that tell us why Olivia could tell that Wuzzy was real.

"What's a Whoowuzzler?" asked Olivia.

"It's an invisible pet," said Sam. "I've called mine Wuzzy."

"And what exactly does Wuzzy look like?" asked Olivia, putting her hand in the box. It was a shock to find that she could feel something small and soft even though she couldn't see anything.

"Well, he kind of looks like a guinea pig but he has feathers instead of fur. His feathers are red, with a few blue ones on his belly," Sam replied.

Olivia slowly felt the creature in the box all over. She had to agree that it was exactly what Wuzzy felt like — a feather-covered guinea pig.

Circle the correct answer for each question.

1. What can we **infer** about Wuzzy from Sam's description?
   - **a** Wuzzy is furry.
   - **b** Wuzzy is colourful.
   - **c** Wuzzy is tiny.
   - **d** Wuzzy is scruffy.
2. Which words are **clues** to question 1's answer?
   - **a** *guinea pig*
   - **b** *kind* and *looks*
   - **c** *feathers* and *fur*
   - **d** *red* and *blue*
3. What other **inference** can we make about Wuzzy? Wuzzy is …
   - **a** a guinea pig.
   - **b** a bird.
   - **c** an unusual creature.
   - **d** a soft toy.
4. Which phrase is the **clue** to question 3's answer?
   - **a** a feather-covered guinea pig
   - **b** creature in the box
   - **c** looks like a guinea pig
   - **d** a shock

AC9E3LY05 Use comprehension strategies to build inferred meaning

Read the passage.

Underline how Zazz moved.

Circle words that tell you that Wuzzy and Zazz were noisy.

Back at home, Zazz grew as fast as Wuzzy had done, but not from eating. The more she bounced the more Zazz grew. And she bounced everywhere! Wuzzy's screeching was no longer the problem. Now it was the thumping of Zazz's long tail.

The only way to stop the thumping was to get Zazz to jump on the bed. When Wuzzy saw how much fun jumping on the bed was, he wanted to do it too. And, when Olivia and Sam saw how much fun their invisi-pets were having bouncing on the bed, they couldn't help but join in.

Highlight four words that suggest that Zazz was getting bigger.

Put a box around the word that names a part of Zazz's body.

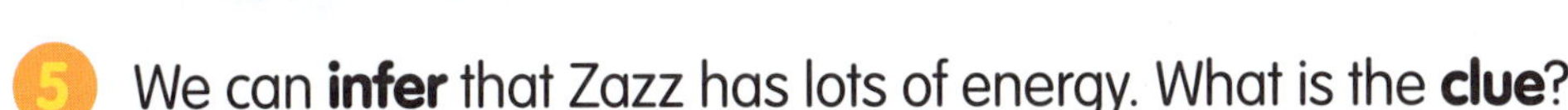

5 We can **infer** that Zazz has lots of energy. What is the **clue**?

6 Which two words **suggest** that Wuzzy and Zazz are noisy creatures?

7 Write a description of Zazz based on **clues** in the text.

8 What does the word *invisi-pets* **suggest** about Wuzzy and Zazz?

9 **How can we tell** that Olivia and Sam enjoy playing with their pets?

LESSON 75

Toothless!

Sequencing Events

To identify the sequence of events in a text, look at numbers and words that give clues to the order in which things happen.

Read the passage.

Underline the first thing Lucy did.

Colour the words that show what Lucy said **while** *Crazy Cleaner* was chugging through the surf.

Underline the question Grandad asked **when** he saw steam coming out of *Crazy Cleaner*.

Grandad and Lucy wheeled *Crazy Cleaner* down to the beach. Lucy set its dials to 'underwater' and 'pickup'. She pushed it into the water and turned it on. *Crazy Cleaner* chugged through the surf.

"Now we'll find your teeth," said Lucy.

"Is it supposed to spurt out steam like that?" asked Grandad. Steam was pouring from *Crazy Cleaner's* engine.

"Oh no! Something's wrong," said Lucy. "Look! It's heading up the beach." *Crazy Cleaner* was chugging over the sand towards them.

"Watch out!" shouted Grandad. They ducked, as *Crazy Cleaner* threw a hat at them and then an umbrella.

Highlight the words that tell us what Lucy did **before** she turned *Crazy Cleaner* on.

Circle the words that show that *Crazy Cleaner* threw the umbrella after the hat.

Number the sentences from 1–7 to show the order in which the events happened.

- [ ] Steam started coming out of *Crazy Cleaner's* engine.
- [ ] Lucy set the dials on *Crazy Cleaner*.
- [ ] Lucy said that something was wrong with *Crazy Cleaner*.
- [ ] *Crazy Cleaner* threw an umbrella at Grandad and Lucy.
- [ ] Grandad and Lucy pushed *Crazy Cleaner* down to the beach.
- [ ] *Crazy Cleaner* chugged through the surf.
- [ ] *Crazy Cleaner* threw a hat at Grandad and Lucy.

AC9E3LY05 Use comprehension strategies to build literal and inferred meaning

Read the passage.

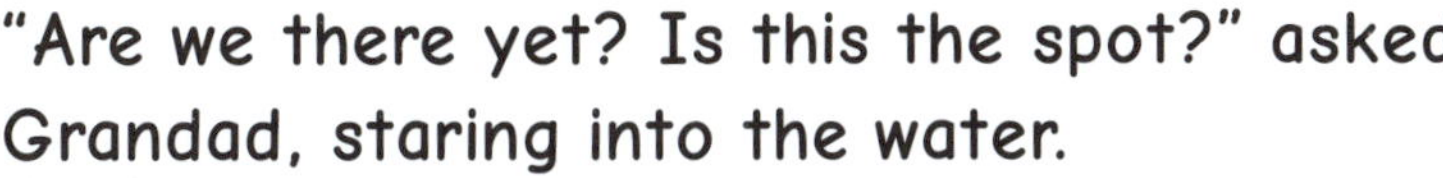

Highlight Lucy's first action.

Colour what Grandad did **after** he grabbed his fishing rod.

"Are we there yet? Is this the spot?" asked Grandad, staring into the water.

Lucy pulled a map out of her pocket and studied it. "Yes, this is it."

Grandad grabbed his fishing rod. He put a prawn on his hook. Lucy grabbed her fishing rod. Then, she pulled a metal box from her pocket. She tied it to the end of her fishing line.

"Isn't that *Doggie's Little Helper*?" asked Grandad. "How's that going to find my teeth?"

"It used to be *Doggie's Little Helper*, but I've fixed it. Now it finds false teeth instead of dog bones," said Lucy.

Underline what Lucy said **while** she studied the map.

Put a box around what Lucy did **before** she pulled the metal box from her pocket.

Write the following events in the correct sequence.

- Meanwhile Grandad put a prawn on his hook.
- Grandad asked if it was *Doggie's Little Helper.*
- Then Lucy pulled a metal box out of her pocket.
- First, Lucy pulled a map out of her pocket and studied it.
- Lucy said she'd fixed it and now it found false teeth.
- She tied the box to the end of her fishing line.

Continuous Tense

The **continuous tense** shows that an action **is**, **was** or **will be happening**. It has a **helping verb** before the **main verb**. For example: *I **am jumping**. She **is hopping**. They **are walking**.* (Present continuous tense) *I **was jumping**. It **was hopping**. We **were walking**.* (Past continuous tense)

Read the extract.

In this sentence, circle the **continuous tense** verb that shows what Leo was doing.

In this sentence, **highlight** the **continuous tense** verb that shows what Leo is doing.

In this sentence, put a box around the **continuous tense** verb that shows what the monsters are doing.

In this sentence, **colour** the **continuous tense** verb that shows what the tears were doing.

Monster Spray

Leo was watching his favourite TV program when his little sister came running into the room.

"Leo! Leo!" she squealed, "come quickly. There are monsters under my bed!"

"Go away, Ruby," said Leo, "can't you see I am watching Pirates on the High Seas?"

"But Leo," whimpered Ruby, "the monsters are sitting under my bed and I'm scared."

Two big tears were running down Ruby's cheeks.

Leo sighed. "Don't worry, Ruby," he said, "I know how to get rid of monsters. Dad's got a special spray that blasts them away. He used it on the monsters under my bed, and they never came back. Wait here for me while I go and find it."

Circle the correct answer for each question.

In the following sentences, which helping verb correctly completes each sentence?

1. Leo ________ watching his favourite TV program.
   a am b are c was d were
2. Leo said, "I ________ watching Pirates on the High Seas."
   a am b is c are d were
3. Ruby said, "The monsters ________ sitting under my bed."
   a am b is c was d are
4. The tears ________ running down Ruby's cheeks.
   a was b were c is d am
5. Leo ________ looking for the special monster spray.
   a am b are c is d were

6 **Each sentence has one word that is incorrect. Circle it, and write the correction in the space.**

- **a** I are trying to make a monster costume. ______
- **b** Olivia were reading a book about monsters. ______
- **c** The little girl are drawing a picture of a monster. ______
- **d** Leo and Ruby is looking for monsters under the bed. ______
- **e** We is planning a monster party for our friend, Leo. ______
- **f** At the party, the children was pretending to be monsters. ______

7 **Which sentence is correct? Tick.**

- **a** ☐ The dog are chasing the boy in the monster costume.
- **b** ☐ The students was looking for information about monsters.
- **c** ☐ I am buying tickets for the new monster movie.
- **d** ☐ The teacher were telling the class a story about monsters.

8 **Choose the correct word to fill each gap.**

The little monster **A** hiding in the cupboard. The other monsters **B** looking for him. The little monster thought, "They **C** taking too long to find me. I **D** getting bored."

A	○ were	○ am	○ was	○ are
B	○ were	○ am	○ was	○ is
C	○ was	○ is	○ am	○ are
D	○ is	○ am	○ are	○ was

LESSON 76

It's a Mystery

Compare and Contrast

When we compare and contrast information, we look for the similarities and differences between details in the text.

Read the passage.

Highlight the CSIs' main job.

Underline the lab-based forensic scientists' main job.

Circle the names of the different types of medical forensic scientists.

Each member of the forensic team has his or her own job.

Crime scene investigators (or CSIs) examine the scene of the crime and collect evidence.

Lab-based forensic scientists carefully analyse this material, often using the latest technology.

Medical forensic scientists, such as pathologists and dentists, are called in if they are needed.

Circle the correct answers.

1. How are members of a forensic team **different**? They …
   - a work in different cities.
   - b wear different uniforms.
   - c do different jobs.
   - d speak different languages.

2. How are CSIs and lab-based forensic scientists **alike**? They both …
   - a examine the scene of the crime.
   - b try to solve a crime.
   - c analyse material using microscopes.
   - d work in a laboratory.

3. How are lab-based and medical forensic scientists **similar**?
   - a Neither uses technology.
   - b Both help CSIs collect evidence.
   - c Both work outdoors.
   - d Both analyse evidence.

4. How are lab-based and medical forensic scientists **different**? Medical forensic scientists are ...
   - a not always needed.
   - b the first ones on the scene.
   - c always needed.
   - d the most important members of the team.

AC9E3LY05 Use comprehension strategies to build inferred meaning

Read the passage.

Underline the similarity between archaeologists and detectives.

Highlight the different things Ötzi might have used his cloak for.

Archaeologists are like detectives. They look for clues too. But they're not looking for clues to a crime; they're looking for clues to the past. The archaeologists called the iceman "Ötzi" and set out to investigate his mystery.

Ötzi was wearing his cloak when he died. It was braided from long grasses and would have been a waterproof layer over his fur clothes. He probably also used it as a blanket or a ground cover.

Colour the different kinds of clues archaeologists and detectives look for.

Circle different materials Otzi's clothes were made from.

5 How are archaeologists and detectives **alike**?

6 How are archaeologists and detectives **different**?

7 What **different** things do archaeologists think Ötzi used his cloak for?

8 What **different** materials were Ötzi's clothes made from?

9 In the following sentence, circle the correct answer.

Otzi's cloak and clothes were both made from natural / synthetic materials.

LESSON 77

TV Guide

Point of View

To identify point of view, we have to look at the way characters act or feel. In reviews, the writer's point of view can be seen in their word choices. Phrases like "I believe" or "we think" tell the reader the information is the writer's opinion.

Read the passage.

Colour the event that made Darren change his mind about his party.

It's Darren's birthday, and he's looking forward to his party until he discovers Mother's bunny decorations! He asks Kerry the goldfish for help, but Admiral Bubbles-in-a-Bowl has other ideas.

Darren Eller Dressed in Yella helps children see foreign lands — in their own rooms. With a new, crazy adventure each week, kids discover that there are magical worlds, full of funny characters, right in their own homes.

Circle two adjectives that help to show the reviewer's opinion of the program.

Circle the correct answers.

1. How does Darren **feel** about his birthday party before he sees the bunny decorations?
   - a He is nervous about it.
   - b He is angry about it.
   - c He is looking forward to it.
   - d He does not want a party.
2. When do Darren's **feelings** about his party start to change?
   - a when he sees his mother
   - b when he speaks to Kerry the goldfish
   - c when Admiral Bubbles-in-a-Bowl arrives
   - d when he sees the bunny decorations
3. Which punctuation helps us to understand Darren's **feelings** about the bunny decorations?
   - a .
   - b ,
   - c !
   - d '
4. In the second paragraph, the reviewer calls the show *funny*. This tells us the reviewer thinks the program is ...
   - a boring.
   - b entertaining.
   - c exciting.
   - d scary.

AC9E3LA03 Describe how texts use different language features and structures

Read the passage.

Underline what the reviewer thinks of the animation.

Highlight the things children can learn from the program.

The animation in this show is always bright, on the go, and very detailed. It doesn't have the homemade look that is popular in children's television these days. As children follow Darren's adventures, they explore everyday emotions, such as love, fear, and happiness, and see how Darren and his family respond to challenges. Highly recommended.

Put a box around the reviewer's overall opinion of the program.

5 Does the reviewer think the animation is good, or bad? Support your answer with evidence from the text.

6 Does the reviewer believe that children can learn something from the program? Support your answer with evidence from the text.

7 Would you recommend this program to someone with a young child? Why, or why not?

LESSON 78

Posters

Drawing Conclusions

To draw conclusions from a text, we have to use clues to make our own judgements. The clues help us find the answers that are hiding in the text.

Study the poster.

Circle the words that tell when the event is.

Put a box around where the event will be.

Highlight the list of legends.

Circle the correct answers.

1. What is the best **conclusion**? Pick in the Park takes place in the …
   a spring. b autumn. c winter. d summer.
2. Which word is the **clue** to question 1's answer?
   a Saturday b February c Park d Pick
3. What is the best **conclusion**? The performance will take place …
   a outdoors. b on a boat. c on a beach. d in a hall.
4. Which word is the **clue** to question 3's answer?
   a legends b Tickets c Pick d Park
5. What **conclusion** can we draw from the list of legends?
   a The concert will be over in minutes. b The concert will run for a few hours.
   c The legends are mainly students. d The legends are mainly teenagers.

6 Which **five conclusions** can we draw from the words and pictures in the poster? Circle the correct answers.

- a Green aliens like to read.
- b There are books on many different topics.
- c Aliens sometimes read scary books.
- d Reading can be exciting.
- e Aliens are wild creatures.
- f People who read are wild.
- g Some books are about unusual things.
- h Libraries have a wide variety of books.
- i Aliens scream when they are scared.
- j There are libraries in most neighbourhoods.

LESSON 79

Forests

Finding the Main Idea and Supporting Details

To discover what a text is about, you need to look for the main idea or key point. Facts and details in the text can help you find the main idea.

Read the passage.

Circle all the names of animals.

Highlight two kinds of forest.

Underline the number of animal species that inhabit a square kilometre in a rainforest.

Put a box around where possums are commonly found.

Forests are full of animals.

There are more insects in a forest than any other type of animal. They make up half the mass of all animal life in a rainforest.

About half of all the world's animal species live in tropical rainforests. Hundreds of bird, mammal and reptile species live in each square kilometre of tropical rainforest.

Most rainforest mammals and reptiles are arboreal. This means they spend most of their lives in trees.

Small animals, such as possums, are common in temperate forests.

Circle the correct answer for each question.

1. What is the passage mainly about?
   - a tropical and temperate forests
   - b different kinds of insects
   - c what forest animals look like
   - d different kinds of forest animals

2. Which sentence best **supports** the main idea?
   - a Most rainforest mammals and reptiles are arboreal.
   - b Forests are full of animals.
   - c This means they spend most of their lives in trees.
   - d They make up half of all animal life in a rainforest.

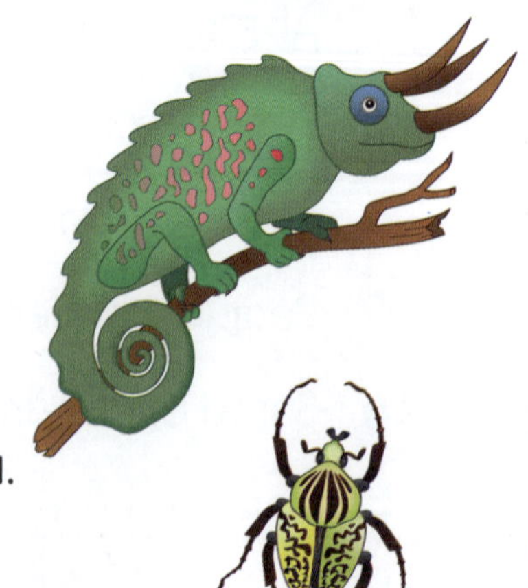

3. Colour the word or phrase that best **supports** the main idea.
   - a mass
   - b insects
   - c live in trees
   - d each square kilometre
   - e bird, mammal and reptile species
   - f common

AC9E3LY05 Use comprehension strategies to build literal and inferred meaning

Read the passage.

In paragraph 1, circle three words that can help us identify the main idea of the text.

Underline the words that tell us what people in forests use plants for.

Forest plants contain chemicals that can be made into medicines.

Plants make these chemicals to protect themselves from diseases, pests and plant eaters.

People living in forests make medicines from plants. They use seeds, leaves, fruits and bark.

Scientists also make medicines from forest plants. The medicines are used to treat asthma, cancer and many other diseases. The drug Taxol, which is used to treat cancer, comes from the bark of the Pacific yew tree.

Highlight the diseases that medicines from forest plants are used to treat.

Put a box around the name of a specific drug that comes from a forest plant.

4 What is the **main idea** or **key point** of the text?

5 Write down **three details** that support the main idea.

a

b

c

LESSON 80

Marsupials

Cause and Effect

To find cause and effect, we ask why something happens and what the result is.

Read the passage.

Underline the reasons bilbies have become a vulnerable species.

Highlight the reason the greater bilby is bred in captivity.

The greater bilby is the largest species of bandicoot. Bilbies are a vulnerable species. Cattle, sheep and rabbits eat the food they need. Foxes and feral cats prey on them.

To save the greater bilby from extinction, they are bred in captivity and then released back into the wild.

Circle the correct answer for each question.

1 What has **caused** bilbies to become a vulnerable species?

- a predators and lack of food
- b diseases and fires
- c air and soil pollution
- d climate change

2 What **effect** has farming had on the bilby population? It has caused …

- a bilby numbers to increase.
- b bilbies to become extinct.
- c bilby numbers to decrease.
- d bilbies to leave their habitat.

3 **Why** are greater bilbies bred in captivity?

- a to keep them safe from foxes and feral cats
- b to make sure they have enough food
- c to try to domesticate them
- d to prevent them from becoming extinct

4 What is the **result** of breeding greater bilbies in captivity?

- a They lose their fear of humans.
- b Scientists can learn more about their habits.
- c They are saved from extinction.
- d They become stronger.

AC9E3LY05 Use comprehension strategies to build inferred meaning

Read the passage.

Underline the reason many Tasmanian devils have died.

Highlight what happens to Tasmanian devils that have tumours on their mouths.

Colour the reason only healthy Tasmanian devils are allowed to breed.

Since 1996, many Tasmanian devils have died from a horrible disease. Lumps grow around the devil's mouth that turn into tumours. These spread across the face and body. The tumours make it hard for the devils to eat. Many starve to death.

Scientists are working to save the Tasmanian devil from extinction. They take healthy devils to wildlife parks. These disease-free animals breed with other healthy Tasmanian devils. In the future, they may be released into the wild.

Circle two adjectives that describe the Tasmanian devils the scientists use in their breeding program.

5 What has **caused** many Tasmanian devils to die?

6 How do tumours on the mouth **affect** the Tasmanian devils?

7 **Why** are scientists making sure only healthy Tasmanian devils breed with each other?

8 What are scientists hoping will happen as a **result** of their breeding program for Tasmanian devils?

GRAMMAR LESSON 4

Noun Phrases

A **noun phrase** is the group of words that is built around a **noun**. It can include **articles** (a, an, the), **pronouns** (e.g. my, his, her), **adjectives** (e.g. big, small) and **other phrases** (e.g. on the wall).

For example: *an enormous giant with a bushy black beard.*

Read the extract.

In the underlined phrase, circle the noun.

In the underlined phrase, put a box around the adjectives.

In the underlined phrase, highlight the pronoun.

In the underlined phrase, colour the article.

Bengal Tigers

Some Bengal tigers live in the mangrove forests of India and Bangladesh.

Tigers hunt mammals such as wild boars. Bengal tigers also eat saltwater crabs and fish.

Tigers are quick and powerful hunters. They have soft foot pads that help them quietly stalk their prey. Their striped coats help them hide in the forest.

Bengal tigers are strong swimmers. They will attack prey while the animal swims or drinks.

Did you know that every tiger has a different pattern of stripes?

Circle the correct answer for each question.

In each sentence, identify the noun phrase.

1 Tigers are able to quietly stalk their prey.

a quietly stalk b are able c their prey d to quietly

2 Tigers are strong swimmers and will attack animals while they drink or swim.

a will attack b they drink or swim c strong swimmers d attack animals

In each underlined phrase, identify the noun.

3 A few Bengal tigers live in the mangrove forests of India and Bangladesh.

a Bengal b few c tigers d a

4 They have soft, spongy foot pads that help them quietly stalk their prey.

a foot b pads c soft d spongy

5 Did you know that the stripes on every tiger form a slightly different pattern?

a pattern b a c different d slightly

AC9E3LA06 Understand that a clause is a unit of grammar usually containing a subject and a verb that need to agree

6 **Complete each noun phrase with a word from the box.**

smell	a	much	of	big

a a large pride ______________ lions

b ______________ tiger in the forest

c ______________ cats like lions and tigers

d an excellent sense of ______________

e a ______________ smaller cat

7 **Which sentence is correct?**

a ◯ The Bengal big tiger is stalking its prey.

b ◯ In the cage was a striped large animal.

c ◯ The small Siamese cat meowed loudly.

d ◯ The lion is an African carnivorous animal.

8 **Each sentence contains two noun phrases. Underline them.**

a We saw a baby cheetah at our local zoo.

b The new movie is about some very funny cats.

c The fluffy white cat is sleeping on the old armchair.

d Our next door neighbour found an abandoned kitten.

e Lions are large, powerfully built cats that live on the African plains.

9 **Make a noun phrase with the following group of words.**

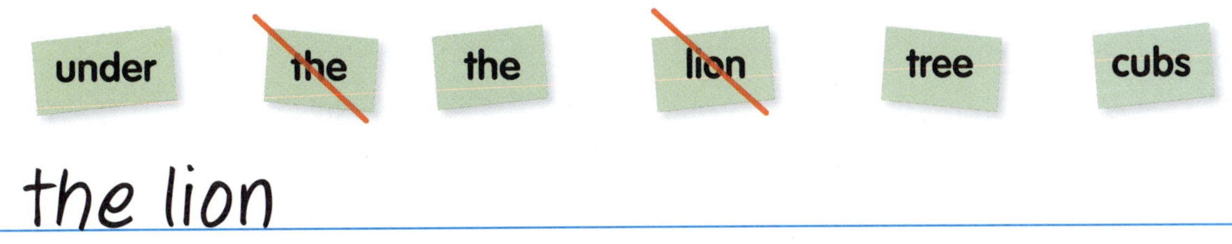

ASSESSMENT 2:

The Great Wall of China

Lexile: 680L

Powerful families called dynasties ruled over ancient China. Each dynasty brought new leaders. The leaders helped the people in different ways. Emperor Qin Shi Huang of the Qin Dynasty (221–206 BC) wanted to keep his people safe.

The Qin Dynasty started to build a wall to keep invaders out. Construction began in 220 BC and took 1726 years to complete. The Ming Dynasty finished it in 1506.

The Great Wall is 7300 km long. It is the longest structure ever built. It runs from east to west along the border between China and Mongolia. The Wall crosses steep mountain ranges and deep valleys.

The Great Wall was built entirely by hand. It is made mostly of earth, brick, wood and stone. Thousands of people worked on The Wall. Many died from injury, disease and starvation.

UNESCO made The Great Wall a World Heritage Site in 1987. It ensures The Wall will be preserved for the future and restored. Thousands of tourists visit every year to see this Chinese treasure.

Circle the correct answer for each question.

1 Which dynasty started building The Great Wall? **LITERAL**

- **a** the Tang Dynasty
- **b** the Ming Dynasty
- **c** the Shang Dynasty
- **d** the Qin Dynasty

2 What is a *dynasty*? **INFERENTIAL**

- **a** way to keep people safe
- **b** rulers from the same family
- **c** an emperor
- **d** servants of the king

3 Why did Emperor Qin Shi Huang start building a wall? **LITERAL**

- a to help travellers
- b to show off his wealth
- c to protect his people
- d to provide jobs

4 How long did it take to complete The Great Wall? **LITERAL**

- a more than 1500 years
- b more than 2700 years
- c more than 2000 years
- d less than 1700 years

5 When was The Great Wall finished? **LITERAL**

- a in 206 BC
- b in 1506
- c in 220 BC
- d in 1726

6 Which are the TWO most likely reasons it took so long to build The Wall? **CRITICAL**

- a Tourists slowed down construction.
- b It was built by hand.
- c It was a complicated design.
- d It was very long.

7 The Great Wall is a World Heritage Site. This tells us that … **INFERENTIAL**

- a everyone should see it.
- b it is an ancient structure.
- c it is a place of great value to the world.
- d it is a popular tourist site.

8 What is the most likely reason many people died while building The Wall? **INFERENTIAL**

- a The workers were very old.
- b The work was hard and dangerous.
- c The Wall was badly built.
- d The workers received no payment.

9 Who is an *invader*? A person who … **VOCABULARY**

- a migrates to another country.
- b is unable to work.
- c attacks and enters a country.
- d is sick and spreads disease.

10 What is the main purpose of this text? **LITERAL**

- a to inform readers about The Great Wall
- b to persuade people to visit China
- c to warn people not to visit China
- d to tell a story about a Chinese emperor

LESSON 81

Chocolate Chuckles

Interpreting Character Behaviour, Feelings and Motivation

To interpret a character's feelings and what causes them to act in a certain way, you need to look for clues in the text. The clues are usually in the words and punctuation.

Read the passage.

Circle words that give us clues about how Mum felt.

Put a box around the phrase that tells us the narrator was relieved about something.

Colour the sentence that shows why the narrator was pleased the kitchen was full of food.

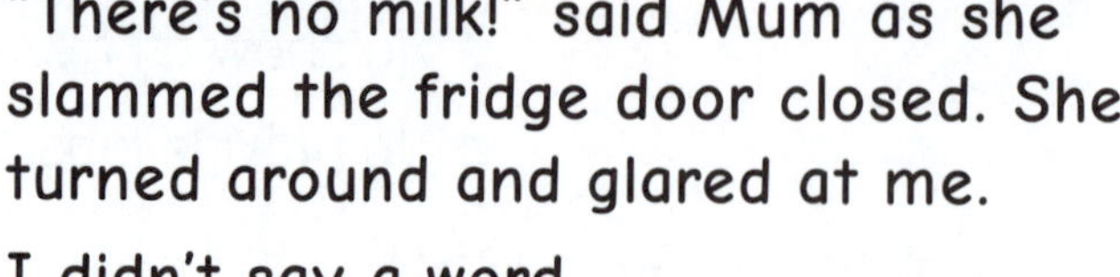

"There's no milk!" said Mum as she slammed the fridge door closed. She turned around and glared at me.

I didn't say a word.

Luckily for me, the kitchen was full of cupcakes, cheese and biscuits, bowls of chips, sausage rolls, pickled onions, streamers, hats and blowers. In the middle of it all was a huge ginger birthday cake with "Happy 80th Birthday" around the edge.

Lucky for me because Mum couldn't see the empty milk carton I'd just been drinking from.

Circle the correct answer for each question.

1. When Mum says "There's no milk!", how does she most likely **sound**?
   - a disappointed
   - b confused
   - c happy
   - d angry
2. Which **word** is a **clue** to question 1's answer?
   - a turned
   - b glared
   - c fridge
   - d milk
3. Which **phrase** is a **clue** to question 1's answer?
   - a slammed the fridge door
   - b turned around
   - c Luckily for me
   - d a huge ginger birthday cake
4. Which **punctuation** is a **clue** to question 1's answer?
   - a .
   - b ,
   - c !
   - d '
5. How would the narrator have **felt** when she realised her mum couldn't see the empty milk carton?
   - a disappointed
   - b confused
   - c relieved
   - d afraid

AC9E3LE03 Discuss how an author uses language and illustrations to portray characters and settings in texts, and explore how the settings and events influence the mood of the narrative

Read the passage.

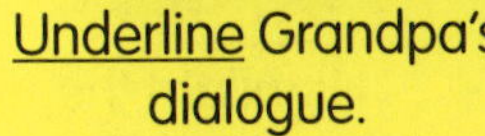

Colour the narrator's thoughts on Grandpa's teeth.

In paragraph 1, highlight the words that show what Grandpa was doing.

Put a box around Grandma's dialogue.

"I'm not going to do it, Mabel," Grandpa was saying. He looked really grumpy and he was shaking his head.

"My teeth are staying in my head until I die." He waggled them with his tongue. They were the most disgusting pair of falsies you've ever seen.

"They're so worn," said Grandma.

"It would be much easier to chew with new ones," said Mum.

6 Which **word** tells us that Grandpa was in a **bad mood**?

7 **Why** was Grandpa in a bad mood?

8 What was the **narrator's opinion** of Grandpa's false teeth?

9 Why did **Grandma think** Grandpa needed new teeth?

10 Why did **Mum think** Grandpa should get new teeth?

LESSON 82

Fairy's Wings

Sequencing Events

To identify the sequence of events in a text, look at numbers and words that give clues to the order in which things happen.

Read the passage.

Circle the scene number.

Underline the first action that happens in the play.

Scene 1 THE GARDEN

Late afternoon. Troy and Tania enter running. Troy has a tennis ball, and they engage in a game of tag.

Troy: Tania! Catch! *Chasing her.*

Tania: Troy ... It's too hard. Throw it softer. *She throws the tennis ball at him. Troy has disappeared.* Troy! Where are you? Give it back. It's my ball.

Troy reappears and torments Tania with her ball. As he does this he falls into a pile of freshly swept leaves.

Highlight the word that tells us that Troy comes back on stage.

Colour Troy's final action.

Circle the correct answer for each question.

1. Which **part of the play** is this?
   - a the beginning
   - b the middle
   - c the end

2. **How do we know** which part of the play it is?
   - a It's late afternoon.
   - b They're in the garden.
   - c It's Scene 1.
   - d They're playing tag.

3. Number the following events to show the **order** in which they happened.
   - ☐ Troy goes off stage.
   - ☐ Troy throws the ball at Tania.
   - ☐ Troy and Tania come onto the stage.
   - ☐ Troy falls into a pile of leaves.
   - ☐ Troy comes back on stage.

AC9E3LY05 Use comprehension strategies to build literal and inferred meaning

Read the passage.

Underline Tania's first action.

Circle the word that tells us that Troy comes back on stage.

Tania bounces the thistledown on the palm of her hand.

Tania: Oh, it tickles.

Mum laughs. Troy re-enters flying a model aeroplane. They collide.

Troy: Tania, watch out!

Tania: Troy.

Troy: You broke the propeller off.

Troy attempts to fix the propeller during the following dialogue.

Tania: Do you think there are such things as fairies, Mum?

Colour the words that show when Tania breaks the propeller.

Highlight the words that show what Troy is doing while Tania is speaking to her mum.

4 In this passage, which is the **first** action that happens?

____

____

5 Which word tells us that Troy has been on the stage **before**?

____

6 What is Troy doing **while** Tania and her mum discuss fairies?

____

____

7 **Complete the following sentence:**

Tania breaks the propeller on Troy's plane **after** ____

____

and **before** ____

____

LESSON 83

Wally the Water Dragon

Finding Facts and Information

To find facts and information in a text, we usually ask the questions **Who? What? Where?** or **When?** The answers can be clearly seen in the text.

Read the passage.

Underline the phrase that tells us where the frogs lived.

Circle what frogs' eggs become when they hatch.

Highlight the sound frogs make.

Once upon a time, we used to have lots of frogs living in our pond. We watched their eggs hatch into tadpoles. The frogs croaked a chorus to us every night. They were especially loud when it rained.

We don't have frogs anymore. We have dragons instead. The dragons ate the frogs' eggs, the tadpoles, and the baby frogs. So the big frogs hopped away to find a safer home.

We still have big goldfish living in our pond. The dragons don't eat the adult goldfish, but I think they eat the babies.

Colour when the frogs croaked especially loudly.

Put a box around the pronoun that shows who thinks the dragons eat the baby goldfish.

Circle the correct answer for each question.

1 **Where** did the frogs used to live?

a beside the river
b among the flowers
c beneath the window
d in the pond

2 **What** do frogs' eggs hatch into?

a goldfish
b dragons
c tadpoles
d baby frogs

3 **What** did the frogs do every night?

a croak
b swim
c sleep
d play

4 **When** did the frogs croak the loudest?

a at night
b in the morning
c when it rained
d in the summer

5 **Who** thinks the dragons eat the baby goldfish?

a the adult goldfish
b the narrator
c the big frogs
d the baby frogs

AC9E3LY05 Use comprehension strategies to build literal meaning

Read the passage.

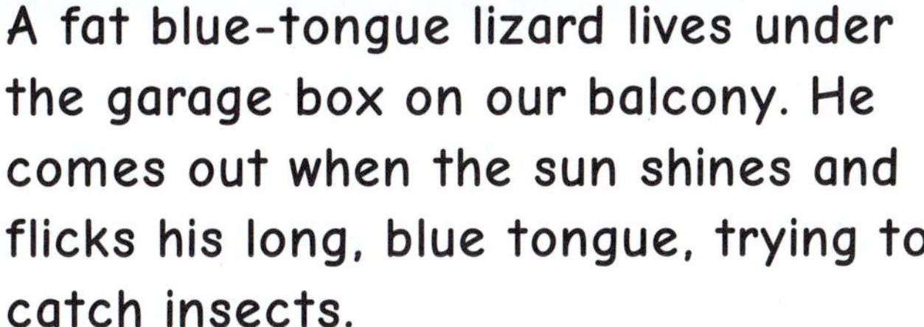

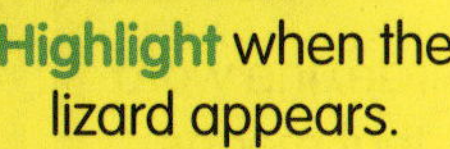

Underline the blue-tongue lizard's home.

Circle the key word that tells us how the blue-tongue lizard catches insects.

A fat blue-tongue lizard lives under the garage box on our balcony. He comes out when the sun shines and flicks his long, blue tongue, trying to catch insects.

Possums hiss in the night and rustle through the trees. They are heading for the banana palms at the back of the house, hoping to find a bunch of ripe bananas for a feast.

Highlight when the lizard appears.

Colour the possums' nighttime behaviour.

6 **Where** does the blue-tongue lizard live?

____

____

7 **When** does the blue-tongue lizard come out of its home?

____

____

8 **How** does the blue-tongue lizard catch insects?

____

____

9 **What** do the possums do at night?

____

____

10 **Where** are the banana palms?

____

LESSON 84

Yellow-bellied Goalie

Point of View

To identify point of view, we have to look at the way characters act and feel. The clues are in the way they express their opinions (what they think and believe) and views about a subject.

Read the passage.

Circle the word that means the same as *scared*.

Underline Ben's thoughts.

Highlight the sentence that tells us what Ben thought of himself.

Colour the word that is similar in meaning to *run away from*.

Ben unpacked the goalie gear from the bag. He pulled on the heavy chest plate, the green-coloured leg pads and the bright orange foot kickers. He put on the safety helmet.

"OK Ben, you're ready for battle," said Coach.

Battle? That's what it was all right.

Ben couldn't move. He was afraid to move. He stood like a statue. He wanted to run away. The only trouble was he could barely walk in his leg pads, let alone run.

He'd be the biggest joke in the team. A giant, padded chicken, trying to escape its fate.

Circle the correct answer for each question.

1. How did Ben **feel** about playing goalie? He was …
   - a excited.
   - b angry.
   - c scared.
   - d happy.

2. Which is the best **clue** to how Ben felt?
   - a He couldn't move.
   - b He felt like a statue.
   - c He was ready for battle.
   - d He wanted to run away.

3. In Ben's **view**, what kind of goalie would he make?
   - a a bad one
   - b a good one
   - c a brave one
   - d a strong one

4. Which phrase helps you see Ben's **view**? He said …
   - a he'd try his best.
   - b he'd be the biggest joke in the team.
   - c he'd act like a giant, padded chicken.
   - d he could barely walk in his leg pads.

AC9E3LY05 Use comprehension strategies to build inferred meaning

Read the passage.

Underline the sentences that show what Ben's teammates said to him.

Highlight a phrase that shows that Ben was proud of himself.

The umpire blew the whistle. The game was over.

"You're a great goalie!" yelled David, patting Ben on the back.

"Benny, you're on fire," cheered another boy.

Ben held his head up high, held his chest out and threw his hands in the air, making high fives with his team.

Ben had done it. He had gone from yellow-bellied to big brave goalie, and it hadn't hurt a bit.

Being a goalie wasn't so bad after all. Maybe, just maybe, he'd give it another go next week.

Circle the word that describes the kind of goalie Ben thought he was before.

Colour two adjectives that describe the kind of goalie Ben thinks he is now.

5. From the **point of view** of Ben's teammates, what kind of goalie is he?

6. In your own words, explain how Ben's **opinion** of himself as a goalie has changed.

7. How does Ben **feel** about playing goalie in the future?

How Owl Got His Feathers

Making Connections

Linking a text to other texts you have read is a great way to build understanding. Look for key words and phrases in the texts to make the connections.

Read the passages.

When the world was young, Owl did not have feathers. One day, all the world's birds decided to hold a grand ball.

"How can I go?" sighed Owl. "All the other birds will wear fine suits to the ball. I have no feathers, and they'll make fun of me."

Hawk heard what Owl had said, and he told the other birds. Every bird gave Hawk a feather, and Hawk passed the feathers to Owl.

Underline the key words in each text that show why the main characters need a special outfit.

Highlight the key words in each text that show why the main characters can't go to the special event.

Colour the key words in each text that show who helped the main characters.

Cinderella gazed sadly at the dying embers in the fireplace. Her stepsister's cruel words rang through her head.

"You can't possibly come with us to the grand ball. Everyone will laugh at you in those miserable rags!"

"But you can go to the ball," said a kind voice. Cinderella gave a start. "I am your fairy godmother," continued the voice, "and I will give you a fine silk gown to wear."

Circle the correct answers.

1 What are the connections between the texts?

- a The main characters have only rags to wear.
- b The main characters want to go to a ball.
- c The main characters are birds.
- d The main characters are given fine silk gowns to wear.
- e The main characters don't have suitable outfits to wear to a ball.
- f The main characters are sitting in front of a fireplace.
- g Kind strangers help the main characters.
- h The main characters are afraid that people will make fun of them.

AC9E3LE02 Discuss connections between character experiences in literary texts

Read the passages.

Owl was so pleased! He flew proudly to the ball.

Owl was having such a wonderful time that he didn't want to give the feathers back, so he silently flew away and hid amongst the trees in the forest.

When the party was over, the other birds looked for Owl, but they could not find him. His new feathers helped him blend into the environment.

Now, Owl only comes out to hunt at night, when the other birds are sleeping.

Circle the word in each text that shows what owls are covered in.

Underline the words in each text that tell us what owls do during the day.

Highlight the words in each text that show how an owl's feathers help to protect it.

Colour the words in each text that tell us what owls do at night.

There are around 200 different owl species. They are nocturnal, which means they are active at night. During the day, they stay hidden in trees.

Most owls hunt insects, small mammals and other birds. Some species hunt fish. Their powerful talons, or claws, help them catch and kill their prey.

Compared to other birds of prey, owls are very quiet in flight. They are hard to spot during the day. Their feathers have a pattern that helps them blend in with the environment.

2 Use the information in the texts to write a short report about owls. Use the headings provided.

Owls

Covering: ______________________________

____

Daytime activities: ______________________________

____

Nocturnal activities: ______________________________

____

Camouflage: ______________________________

____

GRAMMAR LESSON 5

Conjunctions

A **conjunction** is a joining word. A conjunction joins single words in sentences. For example: ***Alex and Isabella are twins.***
A conjunction also joins parts of a sentence. For example: ***I bought a hamburger but I didn't eat it.***
Conjunctions include words like: **although**, **and**, **because**, **but**, **if**, **or**, **so**, **unless**, **until**, **when** and **while**.

Read the extract.

In this sentence, circle the **conjunction**.

Put a box around the **conjunction** in this line.

Highlight the **conjunction** in this line.

In this sentence, underline the **conjunction**.

Box Night News

That night all the neighbours gather in Dave's grandparents' backyard to watch television.

Everyone gathers around the small screen when the news comes on. Nana turns the volume right up so we can hear it over the cicadas.

"This afternoon a young girl went missing from Wattle Grove. Police, firemen and neighbours joined in the search, but it was a young lad by the name of Kevin and his dog Elvis who eventually found her asleep in a bush cave. The little girl was safe and well and was reunited with her family."

"That's me! That's me!" cries Julie when her picture appears.

Circle the correct answer for each question.

Choose the correct conjunction to fill each gap.

1 Everyone gathers around the small screen _____ the news comes on.

a or b when c so d but

2 Everyone can hear _____ Nana turns the volume right up.

a until b because c while d unless

3 Kevin _____ Elvis help the police find the little girl.

a or b so c but d and

4 Police, firemen and neighbours searched _____ they found the little girl.

a while b until c or d although

5 The little girl was sleeping, _____ Kevin and Elvis woke her up.

a or b if c but d because

AC9E3LA03 Describe how texts use different structures

6 Each sentence contains a conjunction. Circle it.

a I can't watch television because I haven't finished my homework.

b She turned up the volume, but I still couldn't hear.

c The TV was too loud, so I asked him to turn down the volume.

d I ate my sandwiches while I watched the news.

e I like programs about animals and the environment.

f He switched off the television when he went to bed.

7 In the following text, choose the correct word to fill each gap.

Police **A** firemen looked everywhere for the little girl, **B** they couldn't find her. They thought they would have a better chance **C** the search party was bigger, **D** they asked the neighbours to join them.

A	◯ but	◯ and	◯ because	◯ so
B	◯ or	◯ unless	◯ so	◯ but
C	◯ if	◯ but	◯ although	◯ until
D	◯ but	◯ unless	◯ so	◯ or

8 Complete the sentences.

a There is a TV in my room, but ______________________________

____

b The neighbours joined in the search for the missing girl because ______________________________

____

c Elvis the dog started barking when ______________________________

____

d Dave's grandad moved the television outside so ______________________________

____

e Every Friday night the neighbours get together and ______________________________

____

LESSON 86

Monsters

Finding Facts and Information

To find facts and information in a text, we usually ask the questions **Who? What? Where?** or **When?** The answers can be clearly seen in the text.

Read the passage.

Circle the name of Japan's favourite monster.

Underline the phrase that tells us where Godzilla used to live.

Highlight the year of the first Godzilla movie.

Colour the words that describe Godzilla's appearance.

Big things are big trouble. Enormous monsters cause chaos and destruction wherever they go. Godzilla is Japan's favourite monster. He first blasted onto Japanese movie screens in 1954 and he's still there today. Godzilla slept on the bottom of the sea until an atomic bomb forced him up to the surface. He looks like a giant *Tyrannosaurus rex* having a temper tantrum. He is angry because he thinks people are destroying the world.

Circle the correct answer for each question.

1. **Who** is Japan's favourite monster?
   - a a giant
   - b a dinosaur
   - c Tyrannosaurus rex
   - d Godzilla

2. **When** did Japan's favourite monster first appear on movie screens?
   - a 1945
   - b 1954
   - c 1956
   - d 1964

3. **Where** did Godzilla live before he was forced into the world?
   - a on an island
   - b in a forest
   - c on the bottom of the sea
   - d in the sky

4. **What** does Godzilla look like?
   - a a huge *Tyrannosaurus rex*
   - b a giant
   - c an angry monster
   - d a sea monster

AC9E3LY05 Use comprehension strategies to build literal meaning

Read the passage.

Underline the words that tell us why people tell monster stories.

Highlight what Native Americans believed dinosaur bones to be.

Circle words that describe Medusa's appearance.

The World of Monsters

Every country has its own stories, or myths, about monsters. Monsters were a good way to explain the unknown. If people didn't know what caused an earthquake, for example, they could say a monster did it.

When Native Americans first dug up dinosaur bones, they thought they were the bones of giant lizards that lived deep in the earth. When these giants shivered, the whole earth quaked!

Many myths tell of monsters with terrible powers. Medusa had snakes instead of hair. Anyone who looked at her was turned to stone. But the hero Perseus was able to defeat her by looking at her reflection in a mirror. Every monster has a weak spot. The trick is to find out where, or what, it is.

Colour Medusa's terrible power.

Underline the actions of Perseus.

Circle the key to defeating monsters.

5 **What** are monster myths used for? ______________________________

____

6 **Where** do people have monsters myths? ______________________________

7 **What** was Medusa's terrible power? ______________________________

____

8 **Who** defeated Medusa? ______________________________

9 **Which** steps will help you defeat any monster? ______________________________

____

LESSON 87

Flowers

Making Connections

Linking a text to other texts you have read is a great way to build understanding. Look for key words and phrases in the texts to make the connections.

Read the passages.

Many animals feed on the nectar from flowers. As a result, the animals carry pollen from flower to flower.

Many insects feed on flowers. Flowers have colour and perfume to attract insects. As insects feed on the nectar, they also pick up some pollen. The pollen catches a ride to the next flower. After being pollinated, flowers make seeds.

Birds, bats and even some lizards are also attracted to flowers.

Circle the word in each text that tells us what insects feed on.

Underline the words in each text that tell us what attracts insects to certain flowers.

Highlight the word in each text that tells us what insects carry from flower to flower.

Colour the words in each text that tell us what flowers produce after they have been pollinated.

Pollination is an important part of the life cycle of plants. Insects such as bees, butterflies and ladybugs are attracted by the bright colours and smells of certain flowers. They know that these flowers contain the sweet nectar that they need to grow and lay eggs. While sucking the nectar, some of the pollen on the flowers sticks to their legs. This pollen gets transferred to the next flower they move to. The pollen fertilises the flower's egg cells to make seeds.

Circle the correct answers.

1. What do both texts tell us?
   - **a** Many insects feed on the nectar from flowers.
   - **b** The bright colours and perfumes of plants help to attract insects.
   - **c** Insects lay their eggs in flowers.
   - **d** Insects play an important role in pollination.
   - **e** Bees and butterflies need nectar to grow and lay eggs.
   - **f** Some flowers grow into fruits.
   - **g** Insects carry pollen from flower to flower.
   - **h** Flowers make seeds after they have been pollinated.
   - **i** Birds and other animals also play a role in pollination.

Read the passages.

Flowering plants are able to live in many different parts of the world. Rainforests, deserts and cold mountains are all home to different flowering plants.

Rainforests get plenty of what plants need — rain, warmth and sunshine — so plants grow in great numbers. A huge variety of flowering plants, such as trees, vines and other tropical plants, grow in rainforests.

<u>Underline</u> all the words in both texts that refer to the climate in rainforests.

Highlight all the words in both texts that refer to the number of plants found in rainforests.

Rainforests cover about 6% of the earth's surface but contain more than half of the world's plant and animal species.

Rainforests have hot, humid climates. They also have a very high annual rainfall. That's why they are called rainforests!

At least two-thirds of the world's plant species grow in rainforests.

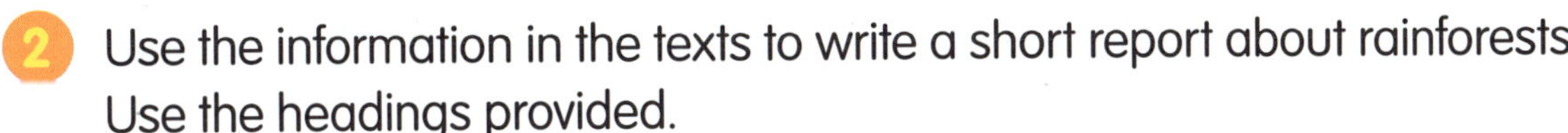

2 Use the information in the texts to write a short report about rainforests. Use the headings provided.

Rainforests

Climate: ______________________________

____

____

____

Plants: ______________________________

____

____

____

LESSON 88

Deserts

Cause and Effect

To find cause and effect, we ask why something happens and what the result is.

Read the passage.

Circle the reason large desert animals are able to stay cool.

Underline the effect a fur covering has on a large desert animal's body temperature.

Desert animals conserve water. They try to avoid very hot and very cold temperatures.

The fur or hair of large desert animals keeps them cool. The outer layer of a camel's coat can be 30 degrees Celsius hotter than its body.

Some desert animals, such as the marsupial mole, burrow underground to escape extreme temperatures. It is cooler underground in hot deserts. In cold deserts, it is warmer underground.

Highlight what the marsupial mole does to stay cool.

Colour the key word that tells why animals in cold deserts might burrow underground.

Circle the correct answer for each question.

1 What **causes** large desert animals to stay cool?

- a their skin
- b their fur
- c their tails
- d river breezes

2 How does a desert animal's hair or fur **affect** its body temperature?

- a It keeps it warm.
- b It causes it to overheat.
- c It keeps it cool.
- d It causes it to freeze.

3 **Why** is the marsupial mole able to stay cool in the desert?

- a It burrows underground.
- b It lies in the shade.
- c It drinks lots of water.
- d It sprays water on itself.

4 What **effect** does burrowing underground have on the marsupial mole? It enables it to …

- a stay warm.
- b find water.
- c find food.
- d stay cool.

AC9E3LY05 Use comprehension strategies to build inferred meaning

Read the passage.

Put a box around the key word that tells us what drilling and mining do to desert environments.

Circle the word that tells us who causes damage to desert water supplies.

Colour the words that show how farm animals damage desert environments.

Deserts often contain oil and iron ore. Drilling for oil and mining can harm desert environments.

Tourists can damage desert water supplies. Vehicles damage desert soils and plants.

When farms are on the edge of a desert, they can damage the fragile desert soil.

Farm animals pound the soil with their hooves. This breaks up the soil. It is then more likely to be eroded by wind and rain.

Highlight the effect vehicles have on desert environments.

Colour the effect farms have on desert environments.

Underline what happens when farm animals break up desert soil.

5 What human activities **cause** damage to desert soils?

6 What **effect** do tourists have on deserts?

7 Explain how farm animals **cause** damage to desert soils.

LESSON 89

Media

Visualisation

Visualising pictures in our heads of the people, places, things and events we are reading about helps build better understanding of the text. Looking for key words in the text will help us create the images in our heads.

Read the passage.

Highlight the words that help you see how the Internet started in the 1960's.

Underline the words that help you see how the Internet spread.

Colour the words that help you see how people use the Internet today.

In the 1960's, a few large computers in the USA connected to each other.

If one of the computers broke down, the others would keep working. Universities began to connect computers in the same way. This grew into the Internet—lots of computers connected to each other.

The Internet spread as more people were allowed to use it. Thousands and then millions of computers went online around the world. The speed at which the Internet sent information got much faster.

Today, billions of people use the Internet to find and share information, for entertainment, and to buy and sell goods.

Read the passage again. As you do so, visualise what you are reading about. Draw pictures of the images as you read about the different stages in the growth of the Internet.

The start of the Internet—the 1960's	More people are allowed to use the Internet

AC9E3LY05 Use comprehension strategies to build literal and inferred meaning

Read the passage.

A storyboard artist turns a film script into a series of drawings to help the people making the story imagine what it is going to look like.

Script for a short film about Humpty Dumpty

Scene 1: *Humpty Dumpty is sitting on the castle wall. He waves to the crowd below.*

Humpty: Hi everyone.

Scene 2: *Humpty stands up. He loses his balance and starts toppling forward.*

Humpty: Aaaaaahhhhhh!

Scene 3: *The people in the crowd look down at Humpty's cracked body. Someone takes out a phone and calls an ambulance.*

Person in crowd: (*talking on phone*) Come to the castle wall quickly. Prince Humpty's had an accident.

Scene 4: *The paramedics patch up Humpty's cracked body.*

Paramedic: You're very lucky, Prince Humpty. If the cracks had been any deeper, you would have needed a yolk transfusion.

Circle the words that help you see what Humpty does in Scene 1.

Highlight the words that help you see what Humpty does in Scene 2.

Underline the words that help you see what Humpty looks like after the accident.

Colour the words that help you see what the paramedics do to Humpty.

Imagine you are a storyboard artist. Create a storyboard for the film about Humpty Dumpty.

Scene 1	Scene 2
Scene 3	Scene 4

LESSON 90

Drama

Finding the Main Idea and Supporting Details

To discover what a text is about, you need to look for the main idea or key point. Facts and details in the text can help you find the main idea.

Read the passage.

Highlight the name of the person who plays an important role in putting on a play.

In paragraph 2, circle all the verbs that tell us what the stage manager does.

Many people work as a team to put on a play. The stage manager has one of the most important jobs.

The stage manager helps the director, actors and stage crew. They plan and run rehearsals and set up the stage. They listen to the actors to check if they are following the script.

When the play is in performance, the stage manager is in charge. They make sure the stage lights go on and off when they need to. They check that the set changes correctly.

The smooth running of the play is the stage manager's responsibility.

Underline the things the stage manager is responsible for when a play is in performance.

Colour the word that describes how the play should run.

Circle the correct answer.

1. What is the passage mainly about?
   - a the director's jobs
   - b the stage crew's jobs
   - c the stage manager's jobs
   - d the actors' jobs

Circle the correct answers.

2. Which three **details** support the main idea?
   - a People work as a team to put on a play.
   - b The stage manager helps the director, actors and stage crew.
   - c The stage manager sets up the stage.
   - d The set changes between scenes.
   - e The stage manager sees that the play runs smoothly.

Read the passage.

Circle the name of Shakespeare's play.

Underline the sentence that tells us about the play's setting.

Colour two sentences that describe what the play is about.

William Shakespeare wrote plays more than 300 years ago. One of his most famous plays is *Romeo and Juliet.*

The play is set in Italy. It is the story of a young man and woman who fall in love. Their families are enemies who don't want Romeo and Juliet to be together. The story has sword fighting, love, sadness and humour.

There have been many interpretations of *Romeo and Juliet*. An interpretation is the way the play is presented. The story and words remain the same, but the setting changes.

The *Romeo and Juliet* story has been used in computer games, songs, operas, ballets and more than 40 films.

Highlight the definition of *interpretation.*

Circle the part of a play that changes with different interpretations.

Underline the different ways in which the *Romeo and Juliet* story has been used.

3 What is the passage mainly about?

____

____

4 List three **details** that support the main idea.

a ______________________________

____

b ______________________________

____

c ______________________________

____

Adverbs of Time

Adverbs of time show:

- **when** an action happens; for example: ***I will see him tomorrow. It happened long ago.***
- **for how long** an action happens; for example: ***I waited all day.***
- **how often** an action happens; for example: ***I sometimes order sushi.***

Read the extract.

Circle the phrase that tells **for how long** people have been making boats.

Put a box around **when** people made simple canoes.

Highlight **when** people built sailboats.

Colour the **adverb of time** in the last sentence.

Boats

People have been making boats for thousands of years.

Long ago, people made simple canoes by carving out logs. They joined wooden or bamboo poles together to make rafts. They used paddles to move these boats.

Later, people built sailboats. Sails catch the wind and push the boat across the water. Sailboats are faster than boats with paddles.

Eventually steamboats replaced sailboats. Coal was burned to heat water. The steam from the water powered the boats.

Today ships are powered mainly by diesel or gas.

Circle the correct answer for each question.

In the following sentences, which word or phrase can replace the underlined adverb?

1. People have been making boats <u>for thousands of years</u>.
   a for a few years b for a long time c for a short time d for many months
2. <u>Long ago</u>, people made simple canoes by carving out logs.
   a In the future b These days c In the past d In a little while
3. <u>Later</u>, people built sailboats.
   a Afterwards b Immediately c Always d Nowadays
4. <u>Eventually</u> steamboats replaced sailboats.
   a In the past b After a while c In the present d At the moment
5. <u>Today</u> ships are powered mainly by diesel or gas.
   a At that time b In future times c In those days d These days

AC9E3LA08 Understand that verbs are anchored in time through tense

6 **In each sentence, circle the word that tells when something happens.**

a I am going sailing tomorrow.

b I will put away the kayak later.

c We will be boarding the cruise ship soon.

d The ship will reach its destination tonight.

e That is the yacht that we sailed on earlier.

f We have finally been allowed to go on board.

g They arrived back from their cruise yesterday.

7 **Colour the word that correctly completes each sentence.**

a Have you ______________ been on an oil tanker?

○ soon ○ before ○ ever ○ now

b My brother ______________ lets me go sailing with him.

○ earlier ○ sometimes ○ later ○ today

c We ______________ managed to start the engine on the boat.

○ eventually ○ daily ○ last ○ ever

d The cruise ship is due to arrive ______________.

○ soon ○ usually ○ never ○ earliest

e ______________ cruise ships could be even bigger.

○ In the past ○ Long ago ○ In the future ○ Every day

8 **Complete each sentence with an adverb from the box.**

always
hourly
yesterday
often
recently

a The ferry departs ____________________.

b I have ____________________ taken up sailing.

c She has ____________________ watched ships entering the harbour.

d ____________________ our class visited the Maritime Museum.

e My father ____________________ wears a life jacket when he goes sailing.

Flight of the Falcon

Lexile: 700L

Geraldine Georgina Jones loved making models. Her room was filled with model ships, dinosaurs, birds, trains and tiny animals. She had just finished painting Falcon on the biggest model plane she had ever made when disaster struck!

A sudden gust of wind swooped through the window. It lifted up the plane and sent it gliding around the room. The plane bumped against her T-Rex, knocking it off the shelf. The T-Rex hit the side of the tall ship. Both ended in splinters on the floor. Geraldine gaped at the mess.

But the wind had not finished its little game. It gathered up her tiny animals and sent them spinning around the room. Geraldine rushed to the window and slammed it shut. Without the wind to hold them up, the animals fell to the floor and broke into even tinier pieces.

Geraldine sat on the floor amongst the broken bits and pieces. The plane glided gently down and landed beside her. She took one look at it and burst into tears.

Circle the correct answer for each question.

1 What was Geraldine's hobby? **LITERAL**

- **a** flying paper planes
- **b** collecting models
- **c** making models
- **d** painting pictures

2 Where was the T-Rex? **LITERAL**

- **a** on top of a cupboard
- **b** on a shelf
- **c** on a desk
- **d** on the window sill

3 What is the most likely reason Geraldine called her model plane *Falcon*? Like a falcon, a plane … CRITICAL

a is silver.
b makes short, high-pitched sounds.
c can make its wings longer or shorter.
d can fly fast.

4 Which of Geraldine's models was T-Rex? LITERAL

a a large bird
b a turtle
c a dinosaur
d a kangaroo

5 Which material did Geraldine use to make the T-Rex and the ship? INFERENTIAL

a wood
b paper
c metal
d cardboard

6 What was the main cause of the disaster in Geraldine's room? INFERENTIAL

a the model plane
b the wind
c the T-Rex
d the tall ship

7 Geraldine gaped at the mess. This means … VOCABULARY

a she took a quick look.
b she stared with her mouth open.
c she giggled.
d she stepped backwards.

8 What happened when Geraldine shut the window? LITERAL

a The tiny animals fell and broke.
b The plane landed on the floor.
c The tiny animals lifted off the shelf.
d Geraldine sat on the floor.

9 Which event happened last? LITERAL

a The dinosaur hit the ship.
b The wind lifted up the plane.
c The models lay broken on the floor.
d The plane bumped the dinosaur.

10 Why do you think Geraldine burst into tears? CRITICAL

____

____

LESSON 91

The Illawarry Cassary

Cause and Effect

To find cause and effect, we ask why something happens and what the result is.

Read the passage.

Put a box around what the narrator did to pretend he was bored.

Highlight the sentence that shows why the narrator almost choked.

Colour the clue to why the narrator called himself an idiot.

Underline what the narrator said when Angus asked to see the bird.

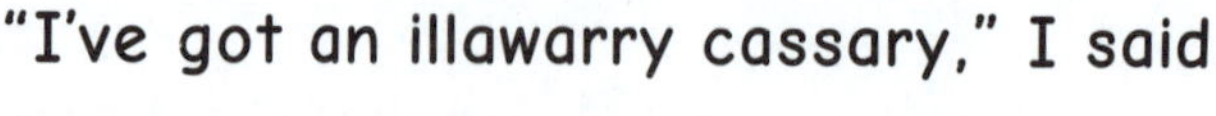

"I've got an illawarry cassary," I said.

Angus eyeballed me. "A what?"

"An illawarry cassary. It's a type of meat eating bird."

"How come," said Angus, still standing with his elbows across his chest, "we haven't heard about this bird before?"

"You never asked," I said, and yawned as if I was really bored.

"We'd like to see it."

I almost choked in mid-yawn. "You idiot!" I was thinking. Of course they'd want to see it.

I thought fast. "It always spits on strangers."

Circle the correct answer.

1. What **happened** when Angus asked why they'd never heard of the narrator's bird before? The narrator pretended to be …
   - a confused.
   - b upset.
   - c surprised.
   - d bored.
2. What **caused** the narrator to almost choke?
   - a gulping in too much air
   - b shock when he heard what Angus said
   - c a tickle in his throat
   - d excitement when he heard what Angus said
3. **Why** did the narrator call himself an idiot?
   - a He'd spoken without thinking.
   - b He should have brought the bird with him.
   - c He should have chosen a different pet.
   - d He was embarrassed about choking.
4. What is the most likely **reason** the narrator said his bird spat on strangers?
   - a to impress Angus
   - b to encourage Angus to come and see it
   - c to stop Angus wanting to see it
   - d to warn Angus not to get too close to it

AC9E3LY05 Use comprehension strategies to build inferred meaning

Read the passage.

<u>Underline</u> what happened just after Emu howled.

Colour why the narrator was surprised when the boys ran away.

Emu gave another howl. In less than a second, I heard three sets of feet running down the driveway.

I couldn't move. What was going on? Surely they weren't scared of a little wet bantam calling out for his dinner? Hadn't they ever seen a chicken before? I stepped forward to go and get Emu in out of the rain, when I suddenly saw it. From where Angus, Martin and Alex had stood, Emu was a two-metre-tall, spiky-feathered, war-helmeted, bloodcurdle-screaming, hungry illawarry cassary!

At school these days we never talk about our pets. And no-one calls me Flake anymore!

Highlight the reason Angus, Martin and Alex ran away.

<u>Underline</u> two things that are different at school these days.

5 What **happened** just after Emu howled?

6 **Why** was the narrator surprised that Angus, Martin and Alex were running away?

7 What had **caused** Angus, Martin and Alex to run away?

8 Name two things that **happened as a result** of the boys seeing the narrator's 'illawarry cassary'.

LESSON 92

Lookout London

Making Inferences

To make inferences while reading, we have to use clues in the text. The clues help us find the answers that are hiding in the text.

Read the passage.

Circle where the parcel was.

Underline how long it will take to get to London.

Highlight why Charles E. Worthington needs help.

Colour two things the wristbands can do.

Hello Will and Vika. You are needed urgently in London, England. Charles E. Worthington needs your help. Something very important is missing. Do not delay. In the corner of the room, under this junk, you will find a parcel containing two transporter wristbands. You must wear these wristbands at all times. They allow you to travel at the blink of an eye and they will keep us in contact.

Remember, this mission is Top Secret. Do not tell anyone you are SWAT agents. You must leave at once.

Circle the correct answer.

1. Which is the best **inference**? Will and Vika are in a …
   - a neat room.
   - b grand room.
   - c big room.
   - d messy room.
2. Which word is the **clue** to question 1's answer?
   - a parcel
   - b junk
   - c important
   - d corner
3. How long will it take Will and Vika to get to London?
   - a hours
   - b weeks
   - c days
   - d seconds
4. Which phrase is the **clue** to number 3's answer?
   - a the blink of an eye
   - b Do not delay
   - c at all times
   - d allow you to travel
5. What is the most likely reason Charles E. Worthington needs Will and Vika's help?
   - a to find out what's missing
   - b to find what's missing
   - c to learn about being a SWAT agent
   - d to find a parcel

Read the passage.

<u>Underline</u> Charlie's description of the West End.

(Circle) the word that means *lots of activity and movement.*

Once across the park they took a shortcut through some of London's old and narrow cobbled laneways. They came out at Piccadilly Circus.

"This part of the West End is the world's theatre capital," said Charlie.

There were signs everywhere saying what was on, what was coming and who was starring. It was a bustle of restaurants, cafes, theatres and cinemas. The three of them walked over to a half-price ticket booth. The lady recognised Charlie straight away.

Colour the places that people can visit in the West End.

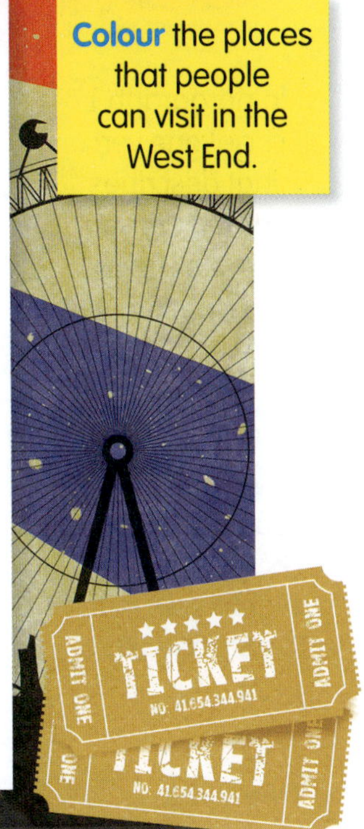

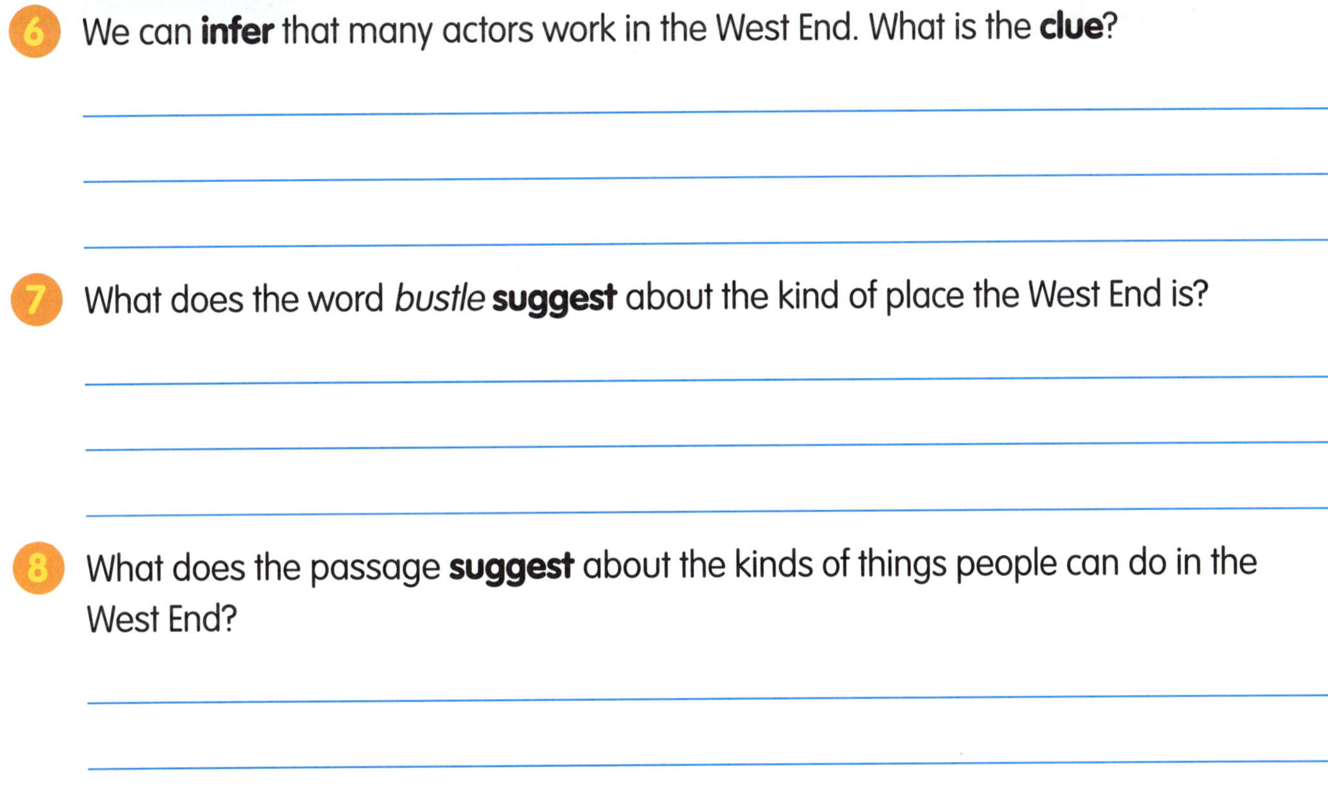

6 We can **infer** that many actors work in the West End. What is the **clue**?

7 What does the word *bustle* **suggest** about the kind of place the West End is?

8 What does the passage **suggest** about the kinds of things people can do in the West End?

LESSON 93

Hedgehogs in the City

Making Connections

Linking a text to events in your own life is a great way to build understanding. Look for key words and phrases in the text to make the connections.

Read the passage.

In paragraph 1, circle one verb that describes something you have done or might do.

In paragraph 2, highlight something you have thrown or might throw in the garbage bin.

Zed and DD, each wrapped in a pickle jar, tipped over and began to roll slowly. The bottled hedgehogs picked up speed, bumping and spinning their way down Garbage Hill.

They skipped over old cars and spun off slimy piles of vegetables, getting air as they hurtled forever downwards.

The two jars collided in midair before landing with a PLUNK! DD's jar smashed into a million pieces. Zed's jar spun on the spot until he popped out, fast as a cork. He shot along the sand, grinding his way to a gritty stop.

In paragraph 3, underline what might happen if you dropped a glass jar.

In paragraph 3, colour what the sand felt like.

Circle the correct answers.

Which of the following have you done, or might you do?

a buy a jar of pickles

b throw an empty pickle jar in the recycling bin

c roll down a slope in a pickle jar

d store things in an empty pickle jar

e roll down a slope

f see a hedgehog

g see a hedgehog in a pickle jar

h play on a garbage heap

i collide with someone

j watch an empty pickle jar smash into pieces

k fall in the sand

l collide with someone while wrapped in a pickle jar

AC9E3LE02 Discuss connections between personal experiences and character experiences in literary texts

Read the passage.

Underline the reason this place reminds the hedgehogs of home.

Highlight the key words that tell us who lives in this place.

The three hedgehogs fell into an oasis: a place that only a hedgehog could dream of. Piles of rotting rubbish filled the air with sweet aromas. It smelt like home.

As the hedgehogs settled on top of the heap, they slowly took in the landscape. Animals of all kinds stared back at them. This was a magical place where all animals were equal and humans did most of the work. "This really is paradise," Ruttel mused.

In paragraph 2, circle an adjective that describes this place.

Colour the word Ruttel uses to describe this place.

The 'oasis' the three hedgehogs land in is a zoo. Carefully read the description of what they see around them.

If you have visited a zoo, write about the things you saw. If you haven't been to a zoo, think of books you have read and write about the things you would expect to see.

LESSON 94

Why Bear Has a Stumpy Tail

Sequencing Events

To identify the sequence of events in a text, look at words that give clues to the order in which things happen.

Read the passage.

Underline the event that happened first.

Highlight the first thing Fox said Bear should do.

Colour what should happen just before Bear gives his tail a strong tug.

Fox saw her friend, Bear. Fox had just stolen a string of fish.

"Can you share them with me?" asked Bear.

"No!" snapped Fox. "Catch your own."

"How can I?" asked Bear. "The lake is frozen."

"Cut a hole in the ice," said Fox. "Then, stick your tail in the lake and hold it there as long as you can. It will hurt when the fish grab it. When you think you have enough fish, give your tail a strong tug to pull out the fish."

Circle the correct answer.

1. Which event happened first?

   a Fox saw her friend Bear.

   b Fox stole some fish.

2. Number the actions to show the order in which they should happen.

   ☐ Fox said that Bear should wait until his tail started to hurt.

   ☐ Fox said that Bear should cut a hole in the ice.

   ☐ Fox said that Bear should pull out the fish.

   ☐ Fox said that Bear should stick his tail in the water.

AC9E3LY05 Use comprehension strategies to build literal and inferred meaning

Read the passage.

Underline what Bear did while Fox watched on.

Highlight the words that show when Bear started pulling at his tail.

Fox watched as Bear put his tail in the water. Then she ran off laughing. Bear thought he felt some fish bite his tail. But what he was really feeling was water freezing around his tail. When the pain got too great, he pulled at his tail. Nothing happened. He pulled harder. He pulled so hard that his tail broke off. All that was left was a little stumpy tail, like bears have today.

Circle the time word in the second sentence.

Colour the sentence that shows what happened after Bear pulled his tail out of the water.

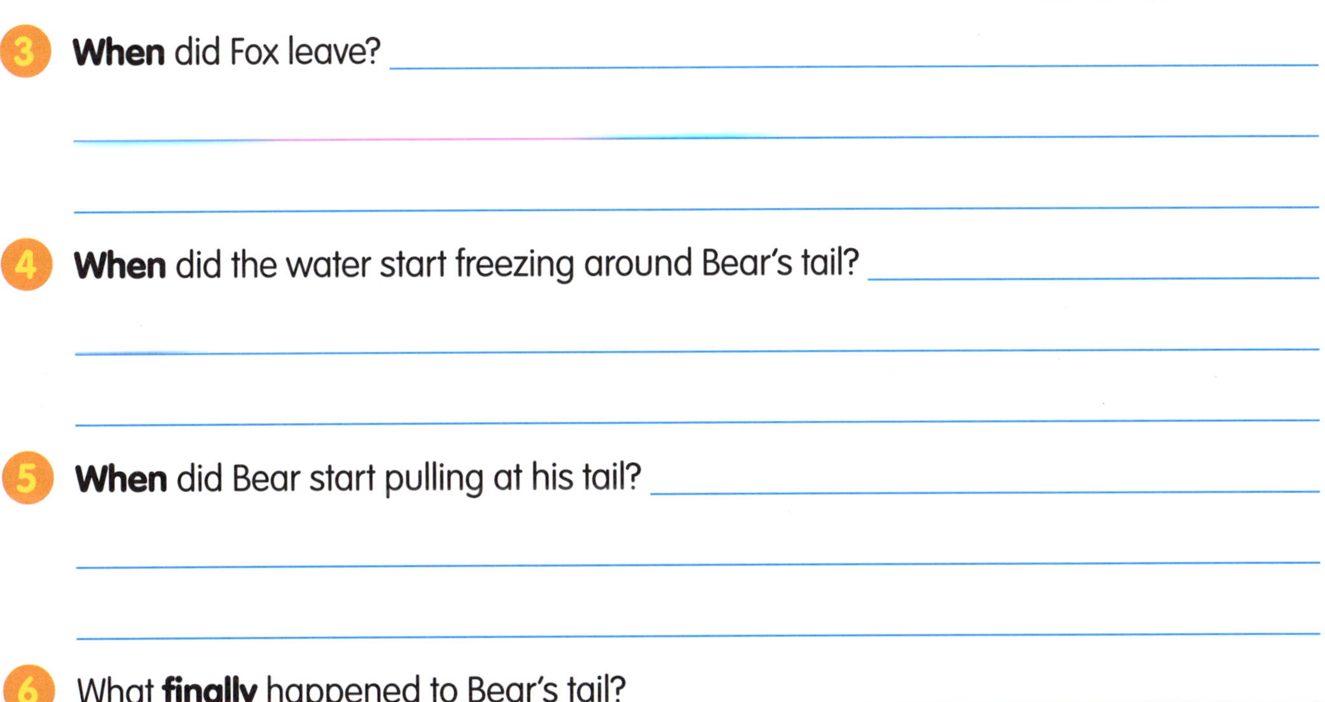

3 **When** did Fox leave? ______________________

____

____

4 **When** did the water start freezing around Bear's tail? ______________________

____

____

5 **When** did Bear start pulling at his tail? ______________________

____

____

6 What **finally** happened to Bear's tail? ______________________

____

____

AC9E3LY05 Use comprehension strategies to build literal and inferred meaning

Limericks

Visualisation

Visualising pictures of the people, places, things and events we are reading about helps build better understanding of the text. Looking for key words in the text will help us create the images.

Read the passage.

Circle the adjective that describes the lady.

Highlight the phrase that describes what the lady's chin looked like.

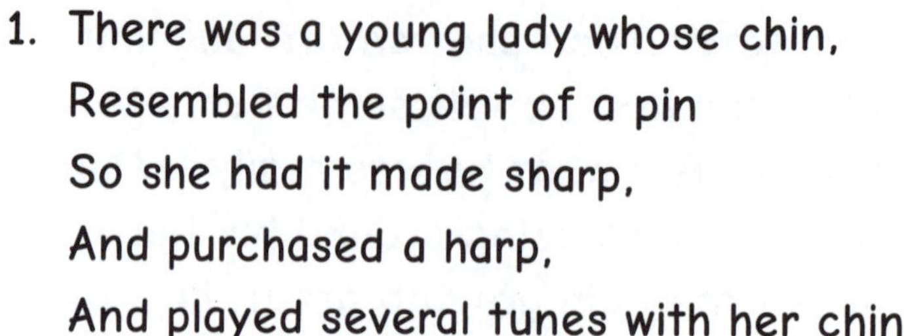

1. There was a young lady whose chin,
   Resembled the point of a pin
   So she had it made sharp,
   And purchased a harp,
   And played several tunes with her chin.

2. There was an old man with a nose,
   Who said, "If you choose to suppose
   That my nose is too long,
   you are certainly wrong!"
   That remarkable man with a nose.

Colour the instrument the lady played.

Circle the adjective that describes the man.

Underline the adjective that describes the man's nose.

Read the poems. As you do so, visualise what you are reading about. Draw a picture of the images as you read each poem.

Poem 1	Poem 2

AC9E3LE03 Discuss how an author uses language and illustrations to portray characters and settings in texts, and explore how the settings and events influence the mood of the narrative

Read the passage.

Circle the word that helped you see what the old man looked like.

Put a box around the word that helped you see what the young lady wore on her head.

1. There was an old man with a beard,
   Who said, "It is just as I feared!
   Two owls and a hen,
   Four larks and a wren,
   Have all built their nests in my beard!"

2. There was a young lady whose bonnet,
   Came untied when the birds sat upon it;
   But she said: "I don't care!
   All the birds in the air
   Are welcome to sit on my bonnet!"

Highlight the words that helped you see the different birds.

Underline the words that helped you see how the lady's bonnet came untied.

Read the poems again. As you do so, visualise what you are reading about. Draw a picture of the images as you read each poem.

Poem 1	Poem 2

Apostrophes and Contractions

An **apostrophe (')** shows where letters have been left out when words are joined together. For example: ***I will help you. I'll help you.***

Read the extract.

Circle the **contraction** of *do not.*

Put a box around the **contraction** of *he has.*

Highlight the **contraction** of *you are.*

Colour the **contraction** of *I will.*

As I was walking home after school that day, I saw Archie and Billy blocking the way of my friend, Li Yong.

"Everything alright?" I asked. I could see plainly that it wasn't.

"Don't try to be a hero like your brother," replied Archie. "We aren't bushrangers. We're just asking your mate here a few questions." He smiled and grabbed a handful of Yong's shirt.

"We think he's found something and we'd like to see it," said Billy. "Archie's been watching Yong slink off up the creek for weeks now. We think he's got himself a secret spot and it might be flowing with gold. Are we right, Yong?"

"You're right," said Yong calmly. "I've been panning for gold. Please—not a word to anyone. Take my pan and tomorrow I'll show you where. It's a very good spot."

Circle the correct answer for each question.

In the following sentences, identify the contraction of the underlined words.

1. I could see that it was not alright.
   a was'nt b wa'snt c wasn't d wasen't

2. "We are not bushrangers," said Archie.
   a are'nt b aren't c arn't d ar'ent

3. We are just asking your friend a few questions.
   a We'are b Wer'e c Wea're d We're

4. "I have been panning for gold," said Yong.
   a I've b Iv'e c I'ave d Ih've

5. "It is a very good spot," said Yong.
   a Its b It's c I'ts d Its'

 AC9E3LA11 Understand that apostrophes signal missing letters in contractions, and apostrophes are used to show singular and plural possession

6 In each sentence, colour the letter or letters that the apostrophe replaces.

a There aren't any gold flakes in the pan.

○ o ○ e ○ a ○ i

b We should've found some gold by now.

○ o ○ a ○ ha ○ hi

c They are sure they'll find gold before the day is out.

○ we ○ i ○ a ○ wi

7 In the following text, choose the correct word to fill each gap.

Soon **A** going to strike it rich. Then **B** live in a big house with a roof that **C** leak and walls that **D** let in the cold.

A	○ we'll	○ we're	○ we've	○ we'd
B	○ we're	○ we'd	○ we've	○ we'll
C	○ doesn't	○ don't	○ didn't	○ couldn't
D	○ isn't	○ won't	○ aren't	○ they'll

8 In each sentence, replace the contraction with a phrase from the box.

It is	**they had**	**he would**	**brother has**
they would	**he had**	**brother is**	**It has**

a He said he'd show them where to find gold. __________

b They wanted to know where he'd been. __________

c It's been too cold to pan for gold. __________

d "It's a long way to the goldfields," said Billy. __________

e They said they'd help us find gold. __________

f I wondered what they'd said to Yong. __________

g My brother's finally struck gold. __________

h His brother's a hero! __________

AC9E3LA11 Understand that apostrophes signal missing letters in contractions, and apostrophes are used to show singular and plural possession

LESSON 96

The First Snowstorm

Point of View

To identify point of view, we have to look at the way characters act and feel. The clues are in the way they express their opinions and views (what they think and believe).

Read the passage.

Underline how the boy feels about the snow.

Circle the punctuation that helps us understand how the boy is feeling.

Colour the words that help us understand how the master feels about the snow.

Farewell, walks to Rivoli! Here is the beautiful friend of the boys! Here is the first snow! Ever since yesterday evening, it has been falling in thick flakes as large as gillyflowers.

It was a pleasure this morning at school to see it beat against the panes and pile up on the windowsills. Even the master watched it and rubbed his hands.

Circle the correct answer.

1. How does the boy **feel** about the arrival of the first snow? He is …
   - a disappointed.
   - b excited.
   - c upset.
   - d nervous.
2. Which phrase in paragraph 1 is a **clue** to how the boy feels?
   - a the first snow
   - b falling in thick flakes
   - c beautiful friend of the boys
   - d since yesterday evening
3. In paragraph 2, which word does the boy use to **express his feelings** about the snow?
   - a beat
   - b pile
   - c pleasure
   - d rubbed
4. How does the master **feel** about the arrival of the first snow? He is …
   - a disappointed.
   - b annoyed.
   - c curious.
   - d pleased.
5. Which phrase is the **clue** to how the master feels?
   - a rubbed his hands
   - b pile up
   - c at school
   - d beat against the panes

AC9E3LY05 Use comprehension strategies to build inferred meaning

Read the passage.

Underline the words that tell us how Stardi felt about the snow.

Put a box around the words that show you how the boys felt.

All the boys were glad when they thought of making snowballs, and of the ice which will come later. Stardi, entirely absorbed in his lessons, and with his fists pressed against his temples, was the only one who paid no attention to it.

What beauty, what a celebration there was when we left school! All danced down the streets, shouting and tossing their arms, catching up handfuls of snow, and dashing about in it, like poodles in water.

6 Explain how the boys **felt** about the arrival of the first snow.

7 How did Stardi **feel** about the arrival of the snow?

8 What does the word **celebration** tell us about how the writer **viewed** the events?

LESSON 97

Plants That Bite Back

Finding the Main Idea and Supporting Details

To discover what a text is about, you need to look for the main idea or key point. Facts and details in the text can help you find the main idea.

Read the passage.

Colour why insects are attracted to the plant.

Circle what causes the insect to stick to the plant.

Each leaf of the sundew plant has hundreds of tentacles. Each tentacle has a drop of sticky liquid on the end. When insects come to drink the nectar, they stick to the liquid. As an insect struggles to get free, the sticky tentacles wrap around its body. Now the plant begins to eat the insect's juicy flesh.

Underline what happens when the insect tries to free itself.

Highlight what finally happens to the insect.

Circle the correct answers.

1. What is the **key point** or **main idea** of the text?
   - a to describe what a sundew looks like
   - b to explain how the sundew traps insects
   - c to explain why insects drink nectar
   - d to show how plants get their food

2. Which three details best **support** the main idea?
   - a The sundew has hundreds of tentacles.
   - b There is sticky liquid on the ends of the tentacles.
   - c An insect comes to drink the nectar.
   - d The insect sticks to the liquid.
   - e The insect struggles to get free.
   - f The sticky tentacles wrap around the insect's body.
   - g The sundew eats the insect.

AC9E3LY05 Use comprehension strategies to build literal and inferred meaning

Read the passage.

Underline how long a giraffe spends eating from a tree.

Highlight what happens when the giraffe starts to eat the leaves.

Colour how long it takes before the leaves become too poisonous to eat.

The giraffes don't eat from one tree for very long. They munch away at a tree for a short time and then they move on.

People watching may think the giraffe is being nice to the tree. The real reason turns out to be very different.

The acacia tree has another way to defend itself — **poison**.

As the giraffe starts to munch on the spiky tree, the tree pushes poison into its leaves. Within 30 minutes the leaves are too poisonous to eat.

Circle the key word that tells us how the acacia tree protects itself from animals that want to eat its leaves.

3 What is the **key point** or **main idea** of the text?

4 Which three **details** support the main idea?

a

b

c

LESSON 98

Mountains

Sequencing Events

To identify the sequence of events in a text, look at numbers and words that give clues to the order in which things happen.

Read the passage.

Circle the key word that tells us how water gets into the cracks.

Colour what happens to the water in the cracks.

Underline what happens after the frozen water expands in the cracks.

Mountains are always eroding. This is mainly due to the effects of ice, rain and wind.

At the tops of mountains, water freezes in cracks in the rock. The water expands when it freezes. It causes the rock to split and pieces to break off. This makes mountains jagged.

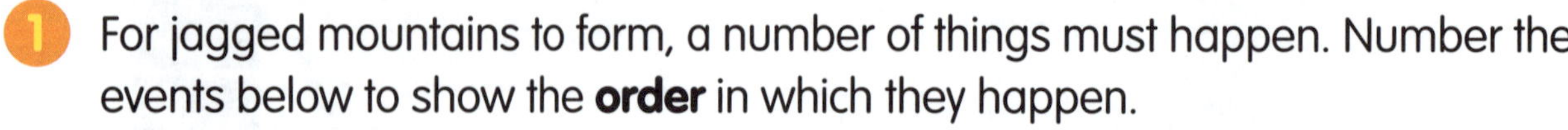

1 For jagged mountains to form, a number of things must happen. Number the events below to show the **order** in which they happen.

- ☐ The rock splits.
- ☐ The rainwater in the cracks freezes.
- ☐ Rain falls.
- ☐ Jagged mountains are formed.
- ☐ At the tops of mountains, cracks form in the rock.
- ☐ Pieces of rock break off.
- ☐ Rainwater trickles into the cracks in the rock.

Read the passage.

Circle **when** the black bear hibernates.

Underline what the bear does before it goes into its den.

Highlight how long the bear spends sleeping.

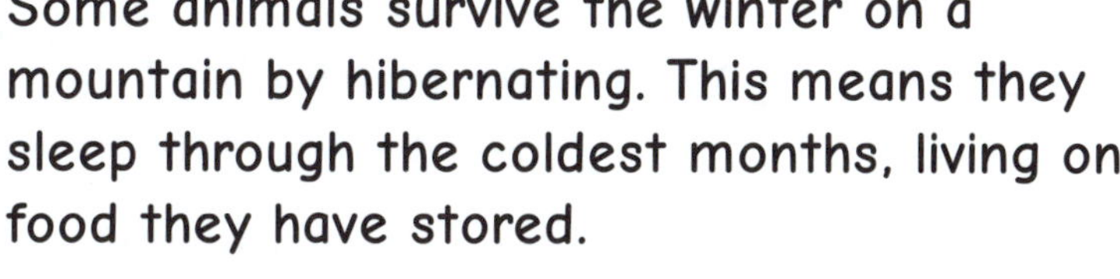

Some animals survive the winter on a mountain by hibernating. This means they sleep through the coldest months, living on food they have stored.

Black bears in the mountains of North America hibernate every winter.

The bear eats as much as possible in summer and autumn. In winter, when there is not much food left, the bear goes into a den to sleep. The den might be a cave, burrow, or the space under some logs on the ground.

The bear's breathing rate drops. It can be as slow as one breath every 45 seconds. It sleeps from four to seven months.

The bear comes out of the den in the spring.

Colour the season that comes after summer.

Underline the season that comes before spring.

Put a box around when the bear comes out of its den.

2 What does the black bear do **before** the winter sets in?

3 What does the black bear do **once** the winter sets in?

4 How long does the black bear stay in its den?

5 Which season comes **after** winter?

AC9E3LY05 Use comprehension strategies to build literal and inferred meaning, and begin to evaluate texts by drawing on a growing knowledge of context, text structures and language features

LESSON 99

Visual Arts

Making Inferences

To make inferences while reading, we have to use clues in the text. The clues help us find the answers that are hiding in the text.

Read the passage.

Underline the sentences that tell us about the liquids used in oil and acrylic paints.

Colour the words that show how long it takes oil and acrylic paints to dry.

Oil paint is pigment mixed with oil. It takes a long time to dry. Acrylic paint is pigment mixed with a synthetic liquid. It looks like oil paint but dries faster.

Watercolour paints are pigment mixed with water. They are used on dry or wet paper.

Some artists mix paint with things such as sand, cement or even straw. This gives the painting an interesting texture.

Highlight the sentence that tells us how watercolour paints are used.

Put a box around the different things artists use to give their painting an interesting texture.

Circle the correct answers.

1. Which is the best **inference**? Oil paint and acrylic paint …
   - a are exactly alike.
   - b are made with different liquids.
   - c both dry quickly.
   - d both take a long time to dry.

2. Which is the best **inference**? Liquid is mixed with pigment to …
   - a bring out the paint's colour.
   - b make the paint dry faster.
   - c give the paint texture.
   - d make the paint easier to apply.

3. From reading the passage, we can **infer** that some artists use paint in creative ways. What is the **clue?**
   - a They use paint on dry and wet paper.
   - b They mix pigment with different liquids.
   - c They mix paint with things like sand, cement and straw.
   - d They mix oil and acrylic paints.

AC9E3LY05 Use comprehension strategies to build inferred meaning, and begin to evaluate texts by drawing on a growing knowledge of context

Read the passage.

Underline the sentence that tells us what a curator does.

Circle the verb that is similar in meaning to *advise*.

A curator cares for a collection of artworks. Every art gallery has a curator.

Curators make sure that artworks are stored and shown properly. They often suggest which artworks the art gallery should buy.

Curators spend a lot of time studying art. They write about art in books.

Curators plan exhibitions. They decide which artworks to put in an exhibition. Some artworks may need to be borrowed from other places. The curator asks to borrow the artworks and organises to have them brought to the gallery.

Colour the sentence that tells us how curators share their knowledge of art.

Highlight the sentence that sums up one of the curator's most important jobs.

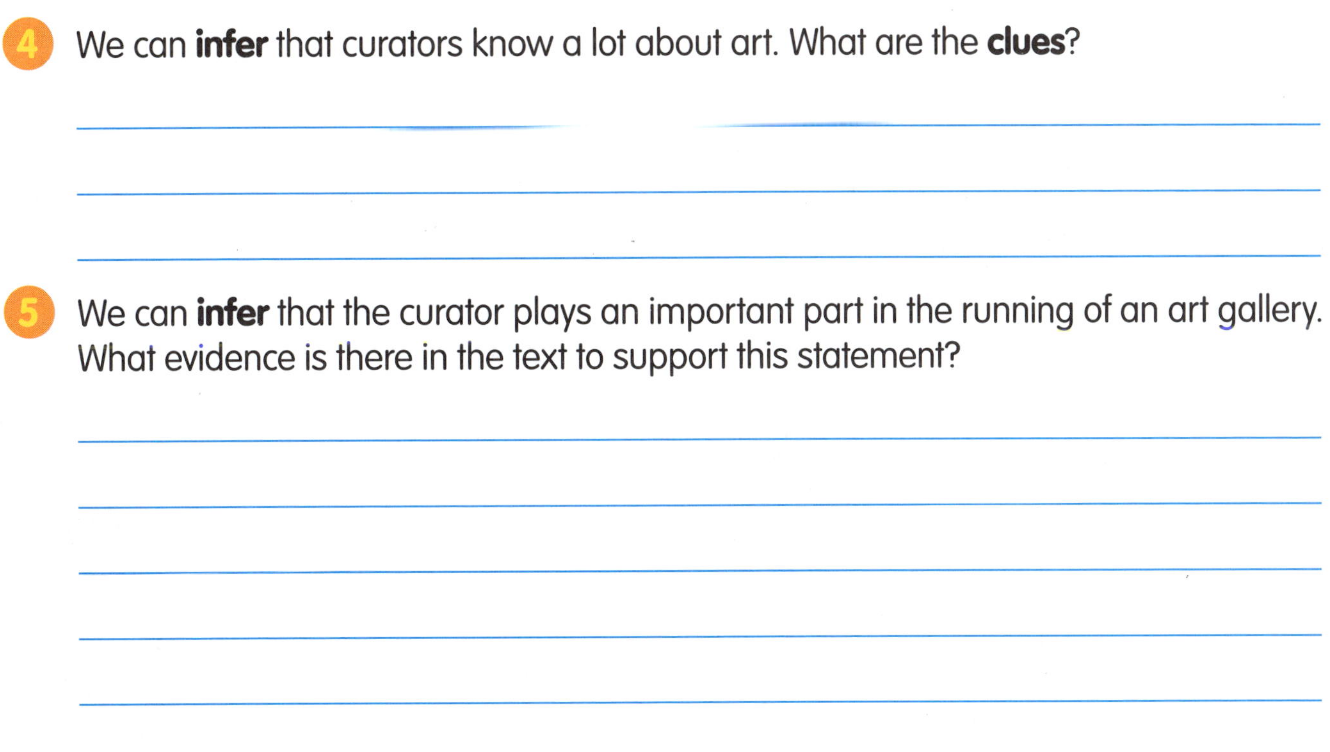

4. We can **infer** that curators know a lot about art. What are the **clues**?

5. We can **infer** that the curator plays an important part in the running of an art gallery. What evidence is there in the text to support this statement?

LESSON 100

Tales of Invention

Point of View

In nonfiction texts, a writer's point of view can be seen in their word choices. Phrases like "I believe" or "we think" tell the reader the information is the writer's opinion.

Read the passage.

Put a box around Ted Wren's opinion of Alexander Graham Bell.

Colour the phrase that gives an opinion of Eliza Bell.

Highlight the words that tell us what most people believe about Alexander Graham Bell's inventions.

Voiceover: Ted Wren continues his series about famous inventors. This week, he looks at Alexander Graham Bell.

I believe Alexander Graham Bell was one of the greatest inventors of the 19th and 20th centuries. He was born in Scotland in 1847. His father, Alexander Melville Bell, was an expert on speech and how the voice works. His mother, Eliza, had poor hearing but many say she played the piano very well.

Alexander Graham Bell moved to the United States in 1871. Five years later he developed the first successful telephone. During his life he took out patents for many inventions, but most people believe that the telephone was his most important invention.

Circle the correct answers.

1. What is the author's opinion of Alexander Graham Bell? Alexander Graham Bell was …
   - a an expert on speech.
   - b an excellent pianist.
   - c a great inventor.
   - d a kind man.

2. Which is an opinion about Eliza Bell? Most people think Eliza Bell …
   - a played the piano very well.
   - b had poor hearing.
   - c was Alexander Graham Bell's mother.
   - d invented the telephone.

3. How do most people feel about the invention of the telephone? Most people believe it was Alexander Graham Bell's most …
   - a dangerous invention.
   - b useless invention.
   - c curious invention.
   - d important invention.

AC9E3LY05 Use comprehension strategies to build literal and inferred meaning

Read the passage.

Underline a sentence that shows that Alexander Graham Bell wanted to help people.

In paragraph 1, circle the key words that show that Alexander Graham Bell had a good imagination.

In 1865 Bell studied how the mouth was used to make sounds and speech. In 1870, the Bells moved to Canada, then America. The next year, young Alexander began to teach at a school for deaf people. He experimented with many inventions. Bell came up with the ideas and his assistant, Thomas Watson, made the equipment. They invented an electric speaking telegraph, which we now call a telephone.

On March 10, 1876, Alexander Graham Bell made the first ever telephone. His diary from that day records, "I then shouted into the mouthpiece the following sentence: 'Mr Watson, come here—I want to see you.' To my delight he came and declared that he had heard and understood what I said."

Highlight the phrase that shows that the telephone was only one of Alexander Graham Bell's inventions.

Colour the phrase that tells us how Alexander Graham Bell felt when he discovered that his invention worked.

4 In your **view**, which of the following words could be used to describe Alexander Graham Bell? You may choose more than one word.

a curious   b lazy   c imaginative   d talented

5 Now explain why you chose those words. Use evidence from the text to support your reasons.

GRAMMAR LESSON 8

Prepositional Phrases

Prepositions often come at the **beginning** of **a phrase** that shows **where**, **when** or **how**. For example:

- Sam went *<u>to</u> the shop*. The **phrase** *to the shop* tells **where** Sam went. The **preposition** is *to*.
- Olivia arrived *<u>at</u> six o'clock*. The **phrase** *at six o'clock* tells **when** Olivia arrived. The **preposition** is *at*.
- Ben walked *<u>with</u> a limp*. The **phrase** *with a limp* tells **how** Ben walked. The **preposition** is *with*.

Read the extract.

Circle the phrase that tells **how** most jobs were done in the 1800s. **Highlight** the preposition.

Put a box around the phrase that tells **where** the personal computer became common. **Colour** the preposition.

Colour the phrase that tells **when** tools will be faster. Underline the preposition.

In the 1800s, most jobs in the home had to be done by hand. Women washed clothes using a washboard. Water was heated in a large metal boiler on a stove.

In the 1900s, factories made new electrical appliances such as vacuum cleaners, washing machines and refrigerators. These appliances made work easier.

Computer technology changed the tools people used in the 1990s. The personal computer became common in homes, offices and schools. Mobile telephones and portable music players also became popular.

In the future tools will be faster, cheaper, stronger and smaller. Nanotechnology is about making tiny tools for science and medicine. Hands-free tools work by voice command.

Circle the correct answer for each question.

1. Which phrase tells **where** water was heated?

   a in the 1800s b on a stove c by hand d in the future

2. Which is the **preposition** in the phrase: *in homes, offices and schools*?

   a homes b and c schools d in

3. Which phrase explains **how** hands-free tools work?

   a by voice command b by hand c by telephone d by themselves

4. In the sentence: *Water was heated in a large metal boiler*, which word is the **preposition**?

   a a b metal c in d large

5. In the phrase: *in the 1990s*, which **preposition** can replace *in*?

   a on b at c during d with

AC9E3LA03 Describe how texts use different language features and structures

6 **Complete each sentence with a preposition from the box.**

a I propped my bicycle ________________ the wall.

b The student is working ________________ her desk.

c He hammered the nail ________________ the wood.

d She ate her food ________________ a knife and fork.

e I downloaded the document ________________ the Internet.

f I haven't used my iPad ________________ yesterday afternoon.

from	with
at	against
into	since

7 **Does the underlined phrase tell *where, when* or *how*?**

a Jack put his tools <u>in the box</u>. ________________

b Their plane gets in <u>at midday</u>. ________________

c Mum cut the pie <u>into four pieces</u>. ________________

d Dad left his phone <u>on the bench top</u>. ________________

e We are travelling to Melbourne <u>by car</u>. ________________

f The electricity went off <u>during the night</u>. ________________

8 **Colour the word that correctly completes each sentence.**

a I bought the batteries __________ the shop.

○ on ○ to ○ at ○ during

b Joe rode to school __________ his new bicycle.

○ on ○ for ○ at ○ by

c We sometimes play computer games __________ school.

○ with ○ after ○ past ○ from

d Ruby found the pencils __________ the drawer.

○ to ○ for ○ in ○ over

e The helicopter hovered __________ the lake.

○ among ○ above ○ under ○ between

ASSESSMENT 4:

The Emu

Lexile: 760L

The emu is Australia's largest bird. It stands about 2 metres tall and has a long, thin neck. Like all birds, it has feathers, two legs and two wings. Unlike most birds, it cannot fly.

The emu has strong, powerful legs. It can run very fast, reaching speeds of over 50 kilometres an hour.

Emus eat berries, wild fruits, caterpillars and grass. They can go for long periods without water, but when they find water, they drink vast amounts. They are good swimmers.

Each year, the female lays between seven and twenty eggs in a nest on the ground. The nest is made of leaves and grass. The eggs are large and greenish-black in colour. The male emu sits on the eggs for up to eight weeks until they hatch. The chicks are striped brown and white, so they are well camouflaged in the grass around them. By six months they begin to look like adult birds.

Emus have good eyesight and hearing. This helps them detect predators such as dingoes, eagles and hawks. When threatened, they defend themselves by kicking out with their strongly clawed feet.

Circle the correct answer for each question.

1 How are emus different from most other birds? Emus … **LITERAL**

- **a** have no feathers.
- **b** cannot fly.
- **c** have no wings.
- **d** lay eggs in nests.

2 Which sentence describes an emu's diet? An emu's diet is a mixture of … **LITERAL**

- **a** nuts and wild fruits.
- **b** grass and berries.
- **c** plants and insects.
- **d** nuts and berries.

3 Which sentence is true? Emus … INFERENTIAL

a do not need to drink water every day.
b cannot run very fast.
c do not have any enemies.
d have poor hearing.

4 When would an emu be most likely to run at speeds of over 50 kilometres an hour? CRITICAL

a when looking for food
b when looking for water
c when escaping from predators
d when chasing its chicks

5 Most birds make their nests in trees. Why do emus make their nests on the ground? CRITICAL

a The nests are too big for trees.
b The eggs are very heavy.
c There is more food on the ground.
d Emus cannot fly.

6 Which emus are eagles and hawks most likely to prey on? INFERENTIAL

a the females
b the males
c old emus
d the chicks

7 Emus may drink vast amounts of water. This means … VOCABULARY

a they drink a little water.
b they do not drink often.
c the water is not clean.
d they drink lots of water.

8 Why is it difficult for predators to see the chicks? The chicks … LITERAL

a are very small.
b cover themselves with leaves.
c blend in with their surroundings.
d hide underground.

9 Dingoes are predators. This means that they … VOCABULARY

a are cleverer than other animals.
b hunt other animals for food.
c stir up trouble.
d are native animals.

10 How does an emu defend itself? LITERAL

____

____

Lesson 61

Pg 2

Later, as Shugg and Katie walked home through the park, Duke stepped out from behind a tree. "Trying to scare me, were you?"

"No," said Shugg.

Duke snatched Shugg's backpack and threw it up into a very tall tree. He stood under the tree with his hands on his hips. "Now let's see you climb up and get it."

1 c **2** d **3** a **4** a **5** a

Pg 3

Peter looked down at the backpack poking out from under the bed. Then he shook his head. "Nah! Not even you would bring home an octopus."

Later that night, Shugg raided the pantry. He found a tin of crab meat and some lobster-flavoured noodles. He opened both and pushed them under the bed.

6 Peter
7 under the bed
8 "Nah! Not even you would bring home an octopus."
9 later that night
10 a tin of crab meat and some lobster-flavoured noodles

Lesson 62

Pg 4

It was Sunday afternoon. I was in my bedroom watching a good movie about aliens when Mum poked her head in. You could tell by the look on her face that she wasn't happy.

"Just look at the state of this room, Jack," she said. "It looks like a pigsty. Turn off the television and clean it up."

"In a minute," I answered, wishing she'd go away. The aliens were about to attack Earth and I wanted to see what was going to happen.

1 c **2** b **3** d **4** a **5** c

Pg 5

I asked Mum where she'd put my lunch. Usually it was on the bench.

"Oh, I don't do lunches," Mum said. "You have to make your own sandwiches."

"I'm already late," I grumbled. "You're going to have to drive me to school."

Mum shook her head. "I don't think so, dear. I don't run a taxi service. You'll have to walk."

Grabbing my school bag, I raced out the door. Thanks to Mum, I didn't have a hope of getting to school on time.

On the way I tried to think of a good excuse to tell my teacher. I decided it was easier to tell Mr Jones the truth.

6 Jack's mum usually made his lunch
7 usually it was on the bench
8 he was going to be late
9 I didn't have a hope of getting to school on time
10 he says, "Thanks to Mum …"

Lesson 63

Pg 6

A good thing about working in the restaurant is being able to choose any dish I like. Shark fin soup is my favourite.

Some customers are funny and have a joke with you. Old people seem to be easier to talk to.

Others aren't so nice. When they order their food, they say things like, "No salt. No soy sauce. Be quick about it."

I'm very careful when taking down their order, so that I get it right.

1 b **2** d **3** c **4** a **5** c

Pg 7

Our school had a Food Day. Mum made me some honey king prawns to take to school.

The principal was very impressed with our Hong Kong food.

On Friday, the principal said, "We're going to visit your restaurant, Kalo. My staff and I will be coming tomorrow night for dinner."

My face went red. I wondered what the principal would order. What if he didn't like the food? What if I dropped a spring roll on him? What would my principal say to Mum? I was not the best student in the school.

6 The principal was very impressed with Hong Kong food.
7 Teacher check
8 Kalo is nervous about the principal and his staff not liking the food
9 my face went red
10 Kalo thinks she is not the best student in the school

Lesson 64

Pg 8

Teacher check passage

1 b **2** d **3** c **4** a **5** d

Pg 9

Teacher check passage

6 he felt very cross
7 The tortoise didn't want to leave home because he was snug and cosy.
8 Teacher check
9 by making the tortoise carry his home on his back for the rest of his life
10 Teacher check

Lesson 65

Pg 10

Narrator: Somewhere on the seven seas is a pirate called Captain Red Beard. The Captain has a ship called The Black Beast. It is a very fine pirate ship. Captain Red Beard and his crew like dropping in on other pirate ships and stealing their treasure.

Fingers: Pirate ship on the starboard bow, Captain.

Captain Red Beard: Good spotting, Fingers. Happy seadogs! Let's meet them.

Ahoy there fellow pirates! Can my crew and I board your ship? We could swap a few pirate tales of terror and treasure.

1 b, d **2** a, c, e

Pg 11

Narrator: Captain Red Beard had an idea.

Captain Red Beard: Nasty? Yes, you are the nastiest pirates I have ever met. We would like to help you be nasty. You must decide on the nastiest thing you can do to us. My crew will go below decks while you have a nasty little meeting about it.

Narrator: Captain Rat thought this was a wonderfully nasty idea. His crew all argued about what was nastiest. Captain Red Beard and his crew went below.

3 he is planning to do something nasty / steal the pirates' treasure
4 they are nasty / they steal treasure
5 Teacher check
6 Teacher check

Grammar Lesson 1

Pg 12

A Country is Born

The caravan in my backyard is the best place to hang out after school. I have all I need in here—a bed, a microwave, even a television.

Knock, knock! I open the caravan door.

"I want to see your school report, Oliver," says Dad, standing on the step. I've been waiting for this. Dad told me weeks ago I must get a good report.

"I've got the best report in the whole school—maybe even Australia," I boast, giving it to him.

"Wow, this is great," he says.

"I know. Suzie is one of the smartest kids in the state."

"Good for her. But I want your report, written about you," he says.

1 b **2** d **3** a **4** c **5** b

Pg 13

6 Teacher check
7 d
8 **a** question?" **b** field,"
9 Teacher check

Lesson 66

Pg 14

Most species of tree are broadleaf trees. They often have flat, wide leaves.

Big, flat leaves can catch lots of sunlight, and they need lots of water. Some broadleaf trees are deciduous and lose their leaves in winter.

Broadleaf evergreen trees, such as holly and orange trees, grow in warmer areas. They do not lose their leaves. Broadleaf evergreen trees have thicker, waxy leaves that often contain oil. The leaves can be large, small, long or short.

Broadleaf trees are flowering plants. New seeds grow from the flowers.

1 d **2** b **3** a **4** c **5** c

Pg 15

Many small mammals live in trees. Trees provide shelter from wind, rain and other animals. Holes in trees become homes for squirrels, and acorns are their food. Koalas live and feed in eucalyptus trees.

Many birds live their lives in trees. They build their nests in the branches or hollows of trees. Trees provide fruits, nectar and seeds for birds to eat.

Millions of insects live in trees. Many types of beetles, ants and butterflies depend on trees for food and shelter.

6 acorns
7 eucalyptus trees
8 in the branches or hollows of trees
9 fruits, nectar and seeds
10 beetles, ants and butterflies

Lesson 67

Pg 16

Stone fruits, fruits with pits, also grow on trees. They have one hard seed covered with soft flesh. Peaches, plums, cherries and apricots are stone fruits.

Many fruits are quite small. Strawberries, raspberries and blackberries are all small fruits with lots of seeds. They grow on small plants or bushes in cool areas.

Apples and pears grow on trees in cool areas. They both have a core with small seeds inside. Some apples are grown to make juice to drink.

1 F **2** T **3** T **4** F **5** T **6** F **7** T

Pg 17

Many animals have a "sweet tooth." Birds and bees drink sweet nectar from flowers, and bears eat honey. People eat sugar made from the dried juice of sugar cane.

Herbs and spices are used in cooking. Herbs such as basil and parsley are used as seasoning. Garlic adds flavour, and chillies are hot and spicy.

Chocolate, vanilla and cinnamon are also plant flavours. Chocolate is made from seeds. Vanilla is made from seed pods, and cinnamon is ground from the dried bark of a tree.

Many drinks are made using plants. Coffee beans and tea leaves both come from plants. Lemonade is made from the juice of lemons.

8 they are both sweet
9 herbs and spices are both used in cooking
10 garlic adds flavour, chilli makes the food hot and spicy
11 Chocolate and vanilla are both plant flavours. Chocolate is made from seeds and vanilla is made from seed pods.
12 Coffee and tea are both drinks. Coffee beans and tea leaves both come from plants.

Lesson 68

Pg 18

Grasslands are environments in which grass is the main plant, rather than shrubs or trees.

Grasslands need 25 to 100 centimetres of rain each year. If they get less than this, they turn into deserts. If grasslands get much more rain, lots of trees grow and they become forests.

There are two main types of grassland — savannas (also called tropical grasslands) and temperate grasslands.

1 c **2** d **3** a **4** b **5** c

Pg 19

The African savanna has cycles of dry and wet seasons.

1 Dry season

Hot winds begin to blow. Grasses die off at the surface, but the roots remain alive. Fires may burn whole areas. Waterholes dry up, causing many animals to migrate. There are often violent thunderstorms before the wet season starts.

2 Wet season

When the rain starts, grass can grow 2.5 centimetres in one day.

6 when hot winds begin to blow
7 they cause grasses to die off
8 because waterholes dry up
9 animals begin to migrate
10 rain during wet season

Lesson 69

Pg 20

Method

1. Turn on the oven to 180° Celsius. Put baking paper on the baking trays.
2. Place flour, sugar, rolled oats and coconut in the bowl.
3. Melt the butter and golden syrup in the small saucepan, and then add bicarbonate of soda and water.
4. Stir the wet mixture into the dry ingredients and mix well.

1 b **2** a **3** c **4** d **5** d

Pg 21

5. Roll teaspoonfuls of mixture into small balls and place on the trays. Leave about 3 centimetres between them.
6. Bake for 10 to 15 minutes. Check the biscuits frequently to make sure they are not burning.
7. Let the biscuits cool slightly before lifting them off with a spatula, to cool on the wire rack.

6 place the balls on the trays 3 centimetres apart
7 bake for 10 to 15 minutes
8 check the biscuits frequently
9 after the biscuits have cooled slightly
10 let them cool on the wire rack

Lesson 70

Pg 22

On April Fools' Day in 1957, an English TV program showed Swiss farmers picking spaghetti from trees. Hundreds of people called the TV station and asked how to grow spaghetti trees. They were told to "place a **sprig** of spaghetti in a tin of tomato sauce and hope for the best".

Because spaghetti was an **exotic** food in England at that time, many people didn't know where it came from. They believed that it could grow on trees!

1 b **2** c **3** d **4** c **5** a

Pg 23

We often believe things we read, especially things that sound scientific. On 1 April 1976, **astronomer** Patrick Moore announced that Pluto would pass behind Jupiter. He said that this would lessen the **gravity** on Earth. If people jumped in the air at the exact moment the planets were in line, they would be able to float—just like astronauts in space. Some people said they had floated up to the ceiling!

6–7 Teacher check

8 He said that this would lessen the gravity on Earth /they would be able to float

9–10 Teacher check

Grammar Lesson 2

Pg 24

Crabs

Most crabs live in the sea. They have a hard, outer shell. The shell protects their soft body.

Crabs have five pairs of legs. The first two legs are claws. The claws are very useful. They hold and carry food. They dig into sand and mud. They crack open shells. They even scare off enemies.

Life in the wild is dangerous for crabs. Many animals prey on them.

Crabs use wonderful tricks to hide themselves. Some hide under rocks and in holes. Others bury themselves in the sand, or are the same colour as their surroundings.

Some crabs dress up to hide themselves. The seaweed decorator crab covers itself with seaweed. It snips off a piece of seaweed with its claws. Then it sticks the seaweed onto its shell. The crab has special hairs on its back. These hairs act like Velcro. They hold the decorations onto the crab's back.

1 c **2** c **3** d **4** c **5** a

Pg 25

6 a live **b** is **c** hatches **d** has **e** are **f** have

7 a Female crabs **b** The young crab **c** Green turtles

8 a eats/eat **b** have/has **c** is/are **d** walk/walks **e** has/have **f** are/is **g** feeds/feed

Assessment 1

Pg 26–27

1 b **2** d **3** a **4** d **5** c **6** a **7** a **8** d **9** d **10** b

Lesson 71

Pg 28

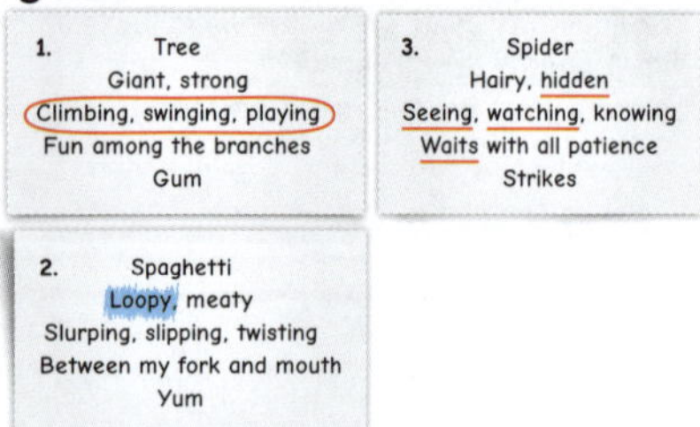

1\. Tree
Giant, strong
Climbing, swinging, playing
Fun among the branches
Gum

3\. Spider
Hairy, hidden
Seeing, watching, knowing
Waits with all patience
Strikes

2\. Spaghetti
Loopy, meaty
Slurping, slipping, twisting
Between my fork and mouth
Yum

Teacher check

Pg 29

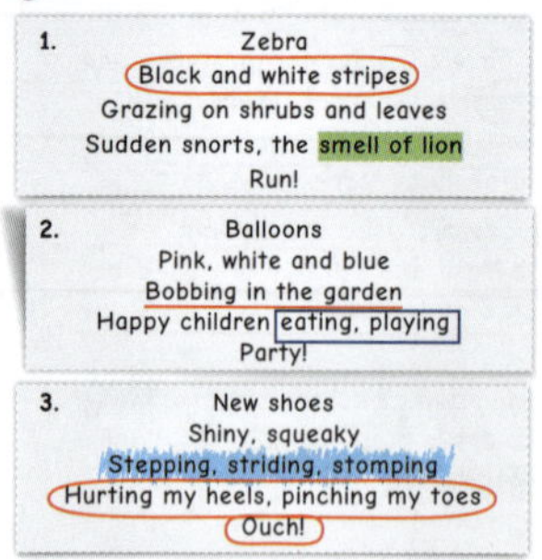

1\. Zebra
Black and white stripes
Grazing on shrubs and leaves
Sudden snorts, the smell of lion
Run!

2\. Balloons
Pink, white and blue
Bobbing in the garden
Happy children eating, playing
Party!

3\. New shoes
Shiny, squeaky
Stepping, striding, stomping
Hurting my heels, pinching my toes
Ouch!

Teacher check

Lesson 72

Pg 30

"Where are you going, Garth?" Mum called as I tried to slip out the front door.

I tried to tell myself it was only half a lie. I was going to Snake's place, I just wasn't staying there.

We sat out the front of his place while I put on my blades.

"Garth, if my mum asks," he said, standing up, "just say we went to the park, okay?" He laughed. "What she doesn't know won't hurt her, right? Come on."

1 d **2** b **3** a **4** c **5** b

Pg 31

"Pay the man, Garth," Snake said.

Luckily I had five bucks on me, so I paid up.

We sat outside in the gutter to eat. We chose a spot so we could watch some builders working nearby.

One of the builders had a dog. He sniffed at us. I offered him a chip.

He liked that and he was coming back for another chip when Snake finished the last of his drink. He threw the can at him.

6 Garth **7** Garth and Snake

8 the dog **9** the dog

10 Snake and the dog

Lesson 73

Pg 32

The Wind and the Sun had a competition to see who could make the man take off his coat. The Wind began to blow as hard as he could. He blew directly on the man with a whipping, punching wind. The man became cold and wrapped his coat closely around his body. No matter how hard the Wind blew, it was useless—the man only held his coat more tightly.

1 b **2** a, c, f

Pg 33

Now it was the Sun's turn. She came out from behind the cloud and shone brightly. The man began to sweat from the heat and decided he could go no further. So he stopped, took off his coat and continued his walk.

3 The sun made the man take off his coat.

4 Teacher check

Lesson 74

Pg 34

"What's a Whoowuzzler?" asked Olivia.

"It's an invisible pet," said Sam. "I've called mine Wuzzy."

"And what exactly does Wuzzy look like?" asked Olivia, putting her hand in the box. It was a shock to find that she could feel something small and soft even though she couldn't see anything.

"Well, he kind of looks like a guinea pig but he has feathers instead of fur. His feathers are red with a few blue ones on his belly," Sam replied.

Olivia slowly felt the creature in the box all over. She had to agree that it was exactly what Wuzzy felt like—a feather-covered guinea pig.

1 b **2** d **3** c **4** a

Pg 35

Back at home, Zazz grew as fast as Wuzzy had done, but not from eating. The more she bounced the more Zazz grew. And she bounced everywhere! Wuzzy's screeching was no longer the problem. Now it was the thumping of Zazz's long tail.

The only way to stop the thumping was to get Zazz to jump on the bed. When Wuzzy saw how much fun jumping on the bed was, he wanted to do it too. And, when Olivia and Sam saw how much fun their invisi-pets were having bouncing on the bed, they couldn't help but join in.

5 she bounced everywhere

6 screeching, thumping

7–8 Teacher check

9 they couldn't help but join in by bouncing on the bed

Lesson 75

Pg 36

Grandad and Lucy wheeled *Crazy Cleaner* down to the beach. Lucy set its dials to 'underwater' and 'pickup'. She pushed it into the water and turned it on. *Crazy Cleaner* chugged through the surf.

"Now we'll find your teeth," said Lucy.

"Is it supposed to spurt out steam like that?" asked Grandad. Steam was pouring from *Crazy Cleaner's* engine.

"Oh no! Something's wrong," said Lucy. "Look! It's heading up the beach." *Crazy Cleaner* was chugging over the sand towards them.

"Watch out!" shouted Grandad. They ducked, as *Crazy Cleaner* threw a hat at them and then an umbrella.

1 4, 2, 5, 7, 1, 3, 6

Pg 37

"Are we there yet? Is this the spot?" asked Grandad, staring into the water.

Lucy pulled a map out of her pocket and studied it. "Yes, this is it."

Grandad grabbed his fishing rod. He put a prawn on his hook. Lucy grabbed her fishing rod. Then, she pulled a metal box from her pocket. She tied it to the end of her fishing line.

"Isn't that *Doggie's Little Helper*?" asked Grandad. "How's that going to find my teeth?"

"It used to be *Doggie's Little Helper*, but I've fixed it. Now it finds false teeth instead of dog bones," said Lucy.

2 Teacher check

Grammar Lesson 3

Pg 38

Monster Spray

Leo was watching his favourite TV program when his little sister came running into the room.

"Leo! Leo!" she squealed, "come quickly. There are monsters under my bed!"

"Go away, Ruby," said Leo, "can't you see I am watching Pirates on the High Seas?"

"But Leo," whimpered Ruby, "the monsters are sitting under my bed and I'm scared."

Two big tears were running down Ruby's cheeks.

Leo sighed. "Don't worry, Ruby," he said, "I know how to get rid of monsters. Dad's got a special spray that blasts them away. He used it on the monsters under my bed, and they never came back. Wait here for me while I go and find it."

1 c **2** a **3** d **4** b **5** c

Pg 39

6 a are/am **b** were/was **c** are/is **d** is/are **e** is/are **f** was/were

7 c

8 A was **B** were **C** are **D** am

Lesson 76

Pg 40

Each member of the forensic team has his or her own job.

Crime scene investigators (or CSIs) examine the scene of the crime and collect evidence.

Lab-based forensic scientists carefully analyse this material, often using the latest technology.

Medical forensic scientists, such as pathologists and dentists are called in if they are needed.

1 c **2** b **3** d **4** a

Pg 41

Archaeologists are like detectives. They look for clues too. But they're not looking for clues to a crime; they're looking for clues to the past. The archaeologists called the iceman "Ötzi" and set out to investigate his mystery.

Ötzi was wearing his cloak when he died. It was braided from long grasses and would have been a waterproof layer over his fur clothes. He probably also used it as a blanket or a ground cover.

5 they both look for clues

6 detectives look for clues to a crime; archaeologists look for clues to the past

7 as a waterproof layer over clothes, as a blanket or ground cover

8 long grasses and fur

9 natural

Lesson 77

Pg 42

It's Darren's birthday, and he's looking forward to his party until he discovers Mother's bunny decorations! He asks Kerry the goldfish for help, but Admiral Bubbles-in-a-Bowl has other ideas.

Darren Eller Dressed in Yella helps children see foreign lands—in their own rooms. With a new, crazy adventure each week, kids discover that there are magical worlds, full of funny characters, right in their own homes.

1 c **2** d **3** c **4** b

Pg 43

The animation in this show is always bright, on the go, and very detailed. It doesn't have the homemade look that is popular in children's television these days. As children follow Darren's adventures, they explore everyday emotions, such as love, fear, and happiness, and see how Darren and his family respond to challenges. Highly recommended.

5–7 Teacher check

Lesson 78

Pg 44

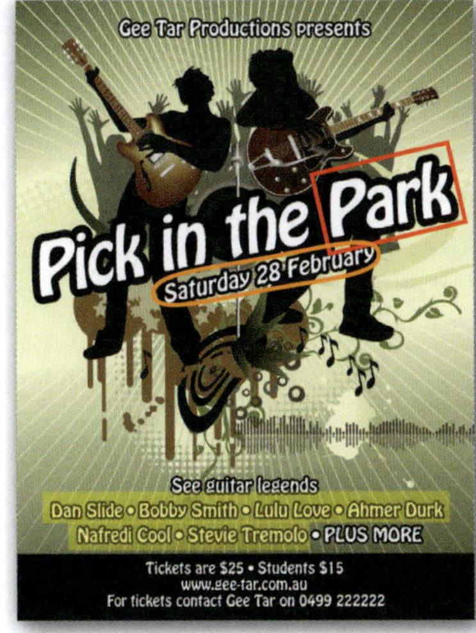

1 d **2** b **3** a **4** d **5** b

Pg 45

6 b, d, f, g, h

Lesson 79

Pg 46

Forests are full of animals.

There are more insects in a forest than any other type of animal. They make up half the mass of all animal life in a rainforest.

About half of all the world's animal species live in tropical rainforests. Hundreds of bird, mammal and reptile species live in each square kilometre of tropical rainforest.

Most rainforest mammals and reptiles are arboreal. This means they spend most of their lives in trees.

Small animals, such as possums, are common in temperate forests.

1 d **2** b **3** e

Pg 47

Forest plants contain chemicals that can be made into medicines.

Plants make these chemicals to protect themselves from diseases, pests and plant eaters.

People living in forests make medicines from plants. They use seeds, leaves, fruits and bark.

Scientists also make medicines from forest plants. The medicines are used to treat asthma, cancer and many other diseases. The drug Taxol, which is used to treat cancer, comes from the bark of the Pacific yew tree.

4–5 Teacher check

Lesson 80

Pg 48

The greater bilby is the largest species of bandicoot. Bilbies are a vulnerable species. Cattle, sheep and rabbits eat the food they need. Foxes and feral cats prey on them.

To save the greater bilby from extinction, they are bred in captivity and then released back into the wild.

1 a **2** c **3** d **4** c

Pg 49

Since 1996, many Tasmanian devils have died from a horrible disease. Lumps grow around the devil's mouth that turn into tumours. These spread across the face and body. The tumours make it hard for the devils to eat. Many starve to death.

Scientists are working to save the Tasmanian devil from extinction. They take healthy devils to wildlife parks. These disease-free animals breed with other healthy Tasmanian devils. In the future, they may be released into the wild.

5 tumours that make the devils starve to death

6 The tumours make it hard for them to eat.

7 to make sure the baby Tasmanian devils are healthy

8 that they are able to save Tasmanian devils from extinction

Grammar Lesson 4

Pg 50

Bengal Tigers

Some Bengal tigers live in the mangrove forests of India and Bangladesh.

Tigers hunt mammals such as wild boars. Bengal tigers also eat saltwater crabs and fish.

Tigers are quick and powerful hunters. They have soft foot pads that help them quietly stalk their prey. Their striped coats help them hide in the forest.

Bengal tigers are strong swimmers. They will attack prey while the animal swims or drinks.

Did you know that every tiger has a different pattern of stripes?

1 c **2** c **3** c **4** b **5** a

Pg 51

6 **a** of **b** a **c** big **d** smell **e** much

7 c

8 **a** a baby cheetah, our local zoo **b** The new movie, some very funny cats **c** The fluffy white cat, the old armchair **d** Our next door neighbour, an abandoned kitten **e** large, powerfully built cats, the African plains

9 the lion cubs under the tree

Assessment 2

Pg 52–53

1 d **2** b **3** c **4** a **5** b **6** b, d **7** c **8** b **9** c **10** a

Lesson 81

Pg 54

"There's no milk!" said Mum as she slammed the fridge door closed. She turned around and glared at me.

I didn't say a word.

Luckily for me, the kitchen was full of cupcakes, cheese and biscuits, bowls of chips, sausage rolls, pickled onions, streamers, hats and blowers. In the middle of it all was a huge ginger birthday cake with "Happy 80th Birthday" around the edge.

Lucky for me because Mum couldn't see the empty milk carton I'd just been drinking from.

1 d **2** b **3** a **4** c **5** c

Pg 55

"I'm not going to do it, Mabel," Grandpa was saying. He looked really grumpy and he was shaking his head.

"My teeth are staying in my head until I die." He waggled them with his tongue. They were the most disgusting pair of falsies you've ever seen.

"They're so worn," said Grandma.

"It would be much easier to chew with new ones," said Mum.

6 grumpy

7 he didn't want new false teeth

8 they were disgusting

9 because they were worn

10 it would make it easier for him to chew

Lesson 82

Pg 56

Scene 1 THE GARDEN

Late afternoon. Troy and Tania enter running. Troy has a tennis ball, and they engage in a game of tag.

Troy: Tania! Catch! *Chasing her.*

Tania: Troy ... It's too hard. Throw it softer. *She throws the tennis ball at him. Troy has disappeared.* Troy! Where are you? Give it back. It's my ball.

Troy reappears and torments Tania with her ball. As he does this he falls into a pile of freshly swept leaves.

1 a **2** c **3** 3, 2, 1, 5, 4

Pg 57

Tania bounces the thistledown on the palm of her hand.

Tania: Oh, it tickles.

Mum laughs. Troy re-enters flying a model aeroplane. They collide.

Troy: Tania, watch out!

Tania: Troy.

Troy: You broke the propeller off.

Troy attempts to fix the propeller during the following dialogue.

Tania: Do you think there are such things as fairies, Mum?

4 Tania bounces the thistledown

5 re-enters

6 Troy attempts to fix the propeller

7 Teacher check

Lesson 83

Pg 58

Once upon a time, we used to have lots of frogs living in our pond. We watched their eggs hatch into tadpoles. The frogs croaked a chorus to us every night. They were especially loud when it rained.

We don't have frogs anymore. We have dragons instead. The dragons ate the frogs' eggs, the tadpoles, and the baby frogs. So the big frogs hopped away to find a safer home.

We still have big goldfish living in our pond. The dragons don't eat the adult goldfish, but I think they eat the babies.

1 d **2** c **3** a **4** c **5** b

Pg 59

A fat blue-tongued lizard lives under the garage box on our balcony. He comes out when the sun shines and flicks his long, blue tongue trying to catch insects.

Possums hiss in the night and rustle through the trees. They are heading for the banana palms at the back of the house, hoping to find a bunch of ripe bananas for a feast.

6 under the garage box on the balcony
7 when the sun shines
8 he flicks his long, blue tongue
9 they hiss and rustle through trees
10 at the back of the house

Lesson 84

Pg 60

Ben unpacked the goalie gear from the bag. He pulled on the heavy chest plate, the green-coloured leg pads and the bright orange foot kickers. He put on the safety helmet.

"OK Ben, you're ready for battle," said Coach.

Battle? That's what it was all right.

Ben couldn't move. He was afraid to move. He stood like a statue. He wanted to run away. The only trouble was he could barely walk in his leg pads, let alone run.

He'd be the biggest joke in the team. A giant, padded chicken, trying to escape its fate.

1 c **2** d **3** a **4** b

Pg 61

The umpire blew the whistle. The game was over.

"You're a great goalie!" yelled David, patting Ben on the back.

"Benny, you're on fire," cheered another boy.

Ben held his head up high, held his chest out and threw his hands in the air, making high fives with his team.

Ben had done it. He had gone from yellow-bellied to big brave goalie, and it hadn't hurt a bit.

Being a goalie wasn't so bad after all. Maybe, just maybe, he'd give it another go next week.

5 He is a great goalie. **6** Teacher check
7 being a goalie wasn't so bad after all

Lesson 85

Pg 62

When the world was young, Owl did not have feathers. One day, all the world's birds decided to hold a grand ball.

"How can I go?" sighed Owl, "All the other birds will wear fine suits to the ball. I have no feathers, and they'll make fun of me."

Hawk heard what Owl had said, and he told the other birds. Every bird gave Hawk a feather, and Hawk passed the feathers to Owl.

Cinderalla gazed sadly at the dying embers in the fireplace. Her stepsister's cruel words rang through her head.

"You can't possibly come with us to the grand ball. Everyone will laugh at you in those miserable rags!"

"But you can go to the ball," said a kind voice. Cinderalla gave a start. "I am your fairy godmother," continued the voice, "and I will give you a fine silk gown to wear."

1 b, e, g, h

Pg 63

Owl was so pleased! He flew proudly to the ball.

Owl was having such a wonderful time that he didn't want to give the feathers back, so he silently flew away and hid amongst the trees in the forest.

When the party was over, the other birds looked for Owl, but they could not find him. His new feathers helped him blend into the environment.

Now, Owl only comes out to hunt at night, when the other birds are sleeping.

There are around 200 different owl species. They are nocturnal, which means they are active at night. During the day, they stay hidden in trees.

Most owls hunt insects, small mammals and other birds. Some species hunt fish. Their powerful talons, or claws, help them catch and kill their prey.

Compared to other birds of prey, owls are very quiet in flight. They are hard to spot during the day. Their feathers have a pattern that helps them blend in with the environment.

2 Teacher check

Grammar Lesson 5

Pg 64

Box Night News

That night all the neighbours gather in Dave's grandparents' backyard to watch television.

Everyone gathers around the small screen when the news comes on. Nana turns the volume right up so we can hear it over the cicadas.

"This afternoon a young girl went missing from Wattle Grove. Police, firemen and neighbours joined in the search, but it was a young lad by the name of Kevin and his dog Elvis who eventually found her asleep in a bush cave. The little girl was safe and well and was reunited with her family."

"That's me! That's me!" cries Julie when her picture appears.

1 b **2** b **3** d **4** b **5** c

Pg 65

6 **a** because **b** but **c** so **d** while **e** and **f** when
7 **A** and **B** but **C** if **D** so
8 Teacher check

Lesson 86

Pg 66

Big things are big trouble. Enormous monsters cause chaos and destruction wherever they go. Godzilla is Japan's favourite monster. He first blasted onto Japanese movie screens in 1954 and he's still there today. Godzilla slept on the bottom of the sea until an atomic bomb forced him up to the surface. He looks like a giant *Tyrannosaurus rex* having a temper tantrum. He is angry because he thinks people are destroying the world.

1 d **2** b **3** c **4** a

Pg 67

The World of Monsters

Every country has its own stories, or myths, about monsters. Monsters were a good way to explain the unknown. If people didn't know what caused an earthquake, for example, they could say a monster did it.

When Native Americans first dug up dinosaur bones, they thought they were the bones of giant lizards that lived deep in the earth. When these giants shivered, the whole earth quaked!

Many myths tell of monsters with terrible powers. Medusa had snakes instead of hair. Anyone who looked at her was turned to stone. But the hero Perseus was able to defeat her by looking at her reflection in a mirror. Every monster has a weak spot. The trick is to find out where, or what, it is.

5 as a way to explain the unknown
6 in every country
7 anyone who looked at her turned to stone
8 Perseus
9 to find out where, or what its weak spot is

Lesson 87

Pg 68

Many animals feed on the nectar from flowers. As a result, the animals carry pollen from flower to flower.

Many insects feed on flowers. Flowers have colour and perfume to attract insects. As insects feed on the nectar, they also pick up some pollen. The pollen catches a ride to the next flower. After being pollinated, flowers make seeds.

Birds, bats and even some lizards are also attracted to flowers.

Pollination is an important part of the life cycle of plants. Insects such as bees, butterflies and ladybugs are attracted by the bright colours and smells of certain flowers. They know that these flowers contain the sweet nectar that they need to grow and lay eggs. While sucking the nectar, some of the pollen on the flowers sticks to their legs. This pollen gets transferred to the next flower they move to. The pollen fertilises the flower's egg cells to make seeds.

1 a, b, d, g, h

Pg 69

Flowering plants are able to live in many different parts of the world. Rainforests, deserts and cold mountains are all home to different flowering plants.

Rainforests get plenty of what plants need—rain, warmth and sunshine—so plants grow in great numbers. A huge variety of flowering plants, such as trees, vines and other tropical plants, grow in rainforests.

Rainforests cover about 6% of the earth's surface but contain more than half of the world's plant and animal species.

Rainforests have hot, humid climates. They also have a very high annual rainfall. That's why they are called rainforests!

At least two-thirds of the world's plant species grow in rainforests.

2 Teacher check

Lesson 88

Pg 70

Desert animals conserve water. They try to avoid very hot and very cold temperatures.

The fur or hair of large desert animals keeps them cool. The outer layer of a camel's coat can be 30 degrees Celsius hotter than its body.

Some desert animals, such as the marsupial mole, burrow underground to escape extreme temperatures. It is cooler underground in hot deserts. In cold deserts, it is warmer underground.

1 b **2** c **3** a **4** d

Pg 71

Deserts often contain oil and iron ore. Drilling for oil and mining can harm desert environments.

Tourists can damage desert water supplies. Vehicles damage desert soils and plants.

When farms are on the edge of a desert, they can damage the fragile desert soil.

Farm animals pound the soil with their hooves. This breaks up the soil. It is then more likely to be eroded by wind and rain.

5 drilling for oil and mining; farming

6 tourists can damage desert water supplies

7 They break up the soil with their hooves, making it more likely to be eroded by wind and rain.

Lesson 89

Pg 72

In the 1960's, a few large computers in the USA connected to each other.

If one of the computers broke down, the others would keep working. Universities began to connect computers in the same way. This grew into the Internet—lots of computers connected to each other.

The Internet spread as more people were allowed to use it. Thousands and then millions of computers went online around the world. The speed at which the Internet sent information got much faster.

Today, billions of people use the Internet to find and share information, for entertainment, and to buy and sell goods.

Teacher check

Pg 73

A storyboard artist turns a film script into a series of drawings to help the people making the story imagine what it is going to look like.

Script for a short film about Humpty Dumpty

Scene 1: *Humpty Dumpty is sitting on the castle wall. He waves to the crowd below.*

Humpty: Hi everyone.

Scene 2: *Humpty stands up. He loses his balance and starts toppling forward.*

Humpty: Aaaaaahhhhhh!

Scene 3: *The people in the crowd look down at Humpty's cracked body. Someone takes out a phone and calls an ambulance.*

Person in crowd: (*talking on phone*) Come to the castle wall quickly. Prince Humpty's had an accident.

Scene 4: *The paramedics patch up Humpty's cracked body.*

Paramedic: You're very lucky, Prince Humpty. If the cracks had been any deeper, you would have needed a yolk transfusion.

Teacher check

Lesson 90

Pg 74

Many people work as a team to put on a play. The stage manager has one of the most important jobs.

The stage manager helps the director, actors and stage crew. They plan and run rehearsals and set up the stage. They listen to the actors to check if they are following the script.

When the play is in performance, the stage manager is in charge. They make sure the stage lights go on and off when they need to. They check that the set changes correctly.

The smooth running of the play is the stage manager's responsibility.

1 c **2** b, c, e

Pg 75

William Shakespeare wrote plays more than 300 years ago. One of his most famous plays is *Romeo and Juliet*.

The play is set in Italy. It is the story of a young man and woman who fall in love. Their families are enemies who don't want Romeo and Juliet to be together. The story has sword fighting, love, sadness and humour.

There have been many interpretations of *Romeo and Juliet*. An interpretation is the way the play is presented. The story and words remain the same, but the setting changes.

The *Romeo and Juliet* story has been used in computer games, songs, operas, ballets and more than 40 films.

3 Romeo and Juliet

4 Teacher check

Grammar Lesson 6

Pg 76

Boats

People have been making boats for thousands of years.

Long ago, people made simple canoes by carving out logs. They joined wooden or bamboo poles together to make rafts. They used paddles to move these boats.

Later, people built sailboats. Sails catch the wind and push the boat across the water. Sailboats are faster than boats with paddles.

Eventually steamboats replaced sailboats. Coal was burned to heat water. The steam from the water powered the boats.

Today ships are powered mainly by diesel or gas.

1 b **2** c **3** a **4** b **5** d

Pg 77

6 a tomorrow **b** later **c** soon **d** tonight **e** earlier **f** finally **g** yesterday

7 a ever **b** sometimes **c** eventually **d** soon **e** In the future

8 a hourly **b** recently **c** always/often **d** Yesterday **e** always/often

Assessment 3

Pg 78–79

1 c **2** b **3** d **4** c **5** a **6** b **7** b **8** a **9** c

10 Teacher check

Lesson 91

Pg 80

"I've got an illawarry cassary," I said.

Angus eyeballed me. "A what?"

"An illawarry cassary. It's a type of meat eating bird."

"How come," said Angus, still standing with his elbows across his chest, "we haven't heard about this bird before?"

"You never asked," I said, and yawned as if I was really bored.

"We'd like to see it."

I almost choked in mid-yawn. "You idiot!" I was thinking. Of course they'd want to see it.

I thought fast. "It always spits on strangers."

1 d **2** b **3** a **4** c

Pg 81

Emu gave another howl. In less than a second, I heard three sets of feet running down the driveway.

I couldn't move. What was going on? Surely they weren't scared of a little wet bantam calling out for his dinner? Hadn't they ever seen a chicken before? I stepped forward to go and get Emu in out of the rain, when I suddenly saw it. From where Angus, Martin and Alex had stood, Emu was a two-metre-tall, spiky-feathered, war-helmeted, bloodcurdle-screaming, hungry illawarry cassary!

At school these days we never talk about our pets. And no-one calls me Flake anymore!

5 three sets of feet ran down the driveway

6 He thought they were scared of a chicken.

7 they were running away from a hungry illawarry cassary.

8 they never talk about their pets anymore, nobody calls him Flake

Lesson 92

Pg 82

Hello Will and Vika. You are needed urgently in London, England. Charles E. Worthington needs your help. Something very important is missing. Do not delay. In the corner of the room, under this junk, you will find a parcel containing two transporter wristbands. You must wear these wristbands at all times. They allow you to travel at the blink of an eye and they will keep us in contact.

Remember, this mission is Top Secret.
Do not tell anyone you are SWAT agents.
You must leave at once.

1 d **2** b **3** d **4** a **5** b

Pg 83

Once across the park they took a shortcut through some of London's old and narrow cobbled laneways. They came out at Piccadilly Circus.

"This part of the West End is the world's theatre capital," said Charlie.

There were signs everywhere saying what was on, what was coming and who was starring. It was a bustle of restaurants, cafes, theatres and cinemas. The three of them walked over to a half-price ticket booth. The lady recognised Charlie straight away.

6 it is the world's theatre capital
7 it is a busy place **8** Teacher check

Lesson 93

Pg 84

Teacher check circle

Zed and DD, each wrapped in a pickle jar, tipped over and began to roll slowly. The bottled hedgehogs picked up speed, bumping and spinning their way down Garbage Hill.

They skipped over old cars and spun off slimy piles of vegetables, getting air as they hurtled forever downwards.

The two jars collided in midair before landing with a PLUNK! DD's jar smashed into a million pieces. Zed's jar spun on the spot until he popped out, fast as a cork. He shot along the sand, grinding his way to a gritty stop.

Teacher check

Pg 85

The three hedgehogs fell into an oasis: a place that only a hedgehog could dream of. Piles of rotting rubbish filled the air with sweet aromas. It smelt like home.

As the hedgehogs settled on top of the heap, they slowly took in the landscape. Animals of all kinds stared back at them. This was a magical place where all animals were equal and humans did most of the work. "This really is paradise," Ruttel mused.

Teacher check

Lesson 94

Pg 86

Fox saw her friend, Bear. Fox had just stolen a string of fish.

"Can you share them with me?" asked Bear.

"No!" snapped Fox. "Catch your own."

"How can I?" asked Bear. "The lake is frozen."

"Cut a hole in the ice," said Fox. "Then, stick your tail in the lake and hold it there as long as you can. It will hurt when the fish grab it. When you think you have enough fish, give your tail a strong tug to pull out the fish."

1 b **2** 3, 1, 4, 2

Pg 87

Fox watched as Bear put his tail in the water. Then she ran off laughing. Bear thought he felt some fish bite his tail. But what he was really feeling was water freezing around his tail. When the pain got too great, he pulled at his tail. Nothing happened. He pulled harder. He pulled so hard that his tail broke off. All that was left was a little stumpy tail, like bears have today.

3 after Bear put his tail in the water
4 when he thought he felt a fish bite his tail
5 when the pain got too great
6 it broke off after pulling too hard

Lesson 95

Pg 88

1. There was a young lady whose chin,
   Resembled the point of a pin
   So she had it made sharp,
   And purchased a harp,
   And played several tunes with her chin.
2. There was an old man with a nose,
   Who said, "If you choose to suppose
   That my nose is too long, you are certainly wrong!"
   That remarkable man with a nose.

Teacher check

Pg 89

1. There was an old man with a beard,
   Who said, "It is just as I feared!
   Two owls and a hen,
   Four larks and a wren,
   Have all built their nests in my beard!"
2. There was a young lady whose bonnet,
   Came untied when the birds sat upon it;
   But she said: "I don't care!
   All the birds in the air
   Are welcome to sit on my bonnet!"

Teacher check

Grammar Lesson 7

Pg 90

As I was walking home after school that day, I saw Archie and Billy blocking the way of my friend, Li Yong.

"Everything alright?" I asked. I could see plainly that it wasn't.

"Don't try to be a hero like your brother," replied Archie. "We aren't bushrangers. We're just asking your mate here a few questions." He smiled and grabbed a handful of Yong's shirt.

"We think he's found something and we'd like to see it," said Billy. "Archie's been watching Yong slink off up the creek for weeks now. We think he's got himself a secret spot and it might be flowing with gold. Are we right, Yong?"

"You're right," said Yong calmly. "I've been panning for gold. Please—not a word to anyone. Take my pan and tomorrow I'll show you where. It's a very good spot."

1 c **2** b **3** d **4** a **5** b

Pg 91

6 a o **b** ha **c** wi
7 A we're **B** we'll **C** doesn't **D** won't
8 a he would **b** he had **c** It has **d** It is **e** they would **f** they had **g** brother has **h** brother is

Lesson 96

Pg 92

Farewell, walks to Rivoli! Here is the beautiful friend of the boys! Here is the first snow! Ever since yesterday evening, it has been falling in thick flakes as large as gillyflowers.

It was a pleasure this morning at school to see it beat against the panes and pile up on the windowsills. Even the master watched it and rubbed his hands.

1 b **2** c **3** c **4** d **5** a

Pg 93

All the boys were glad when they thought of making snowballs, and of the ice which will come later. Stardi, entirely absorbed in his lessons, and with his fists pressed against his temples, was the only one who paid no attention to it.

What beauty, what a celebration there was when we left school! All danced down the streets, shouting and tossing their arms, catching up handfuls of snow, and dashing about in it, like poodles in water.

6–8 Teacher check

Lesson 97

Pg 94

Each leaf of the sundew plant has hundreds of tentacles. Each tentacle has a drop of sticky liquid on the end. When insects come to drink the nectar, they stick to the liquid. As an insect struggles to get free, the sticky tentacles wrap around its body. Now the plant begins to eat the insect's juicy flesh.

1 b **2** b, d, f

ANSWERS • PAGES 95–105

Pg 95

The giraffes don't eat from one tree for very long. They munch away at a tree for a short time and then they move on.

People watching may think the giraffe is being nice to the tree. The real reason turns out to be very different.

The acacia tree has another way to defend itself —poison

As the giraffe starts to munch on the spiky tree, the tree pushes poison into its leaves. Within 30 minutes the leaves are too poisonous to eat.

3 the acacia tree can only be eaten for 30 mins before it becomes poisonous

4 Teacher check

Lesson 98

Pg 96

Mountains are always eroding. This is mainly due to the effects of ice, rain and wind.

At the tops of mountains, water freezes in cracks in the rock. The water expands when it freezes. It causes the rock to split and pieces break off. This makes mountains jagged.

1 5, 4, 2, 7, 1, 6, 3

Pg 97

Some animals survive the winter on a mountain by hibernating. This means they sleep through the coldest months, living on food they have stored.

Black bears in the mountains of North America hibernate every winter.

The bear eats as much as possible in summer and autumn. In winter, when there is not much food left, the bear goes into a den to sleep. The den might be a cave, burrow, or the space under some logs on the ground.

The bear's breathing rate drops. It can be as slow as one breath every 45 seconds. It sleeps from four to seven months.

The bear comes out of the den in the spring.

2 it eats as much as possible in summer and autumn

3 it goes into a den to sleep

4 four to seven months

5 spring

Lesson 99

Pg 98

Oil paint is pigment mixed with oil. It takes a long time to dry. Acrylic paint is pigment mixed with a synthetic liquid. It looks like oil paint but dries faster.

Watercolour paints are pigment mixed with water. They are used on dry or wet paper.

Some artists mix paint with things such as sand, cement or even straw. This gives the painting an interesting texture.

1 b **2** a **3** c

Pg 99

A curator cares for a collection of artworks. Every art gallery has a curator.

Curators make sure that artworks are stored and shown properly. They often suggest which artworks the art gallery should buy.

Curators spend a lot of time studying art. They write about art in books. Curators plan exhibitions. They decide which artworks to put in an exhibition. Some artworks may need to be borrowed from other places. The curator asks to borrow the artworks and organises to have them brought to the gallery.

4–5 Teacher check

Lesson 100

Pg 100

Voiceover: Ted Wren continues his series about famous inventors. This week, he looks at Alexander Graham Bell.

I believe Alexander Graham Bell was one of the greatest inventors of the 19th and 20th centuries. He was born in Scotland in 1847. His father, Alexander Melville Bell, was an expert on speech and how the voice works. His mother, Eliza, had poor hearing but many say she played the piano very well. Alexander Graham Bell moved to the United States in 1871. Five years later he developed the first successful telephone. During his life he took out patents for many inventions, but most people believe that the telephone was his most important invention.

1 c **2** a **3** d

Pg 101

In 1865 Bell studied how the mouth was used to make sounds and speech. In 1870, the Bells moved to Canada, then America. The next year, young Alexander began to teach at a school for deaf people. He experimented with many inventions. Bell came up with the ideas and his assistant, Thomas Watson, made the equipment. They invented an electric speaking telegraph, which we now call a telephone.

On March 10, 1876, Alexander Graham Bell made the first ever telephone. His diary from that day records, "I then shouted into the mouthpiece the following sentence: 'Mr Watson, come here—I want to see you.' To my delight he came and declared that he had heard and understood what I said."

4–5 Teacher check

Grammar Lesson 8

Pg 102

In the 1800s, most jobs in the home had to be done by hand. Women washed clothes using a washboard. Water was heated in a large metal boiler on a stove.

In the 1900s, factories made new electrical appliances such as vacuum cleaners, washing machines and refrigerators. These appliances made work easier.

Computer technology changed the tools people used in the 1990s. The personal computer became common in homes, offices and schools. Mobile telephones and portable music players also became popular.

In the future tools will be faster, cheaper, stronger and smaller. Nanotechnology is about making tiny tools for science and medicine. Hands-free tools work by voice command.

1 b **2** d **3** a **4** c **5** c

Pg 103

6 a against **b** at **c** into **d** with **e** from **f** since

7 a where **b** when **c** how **d** where **e** how **f** when

8 a at **b** on **c** after **d** in **e** above

Assessment 4

Pg 104–105

1 b **2** b **3** a **4** a **5** d **6** d **7** d **8** c **9** b

10 by kicking out with their strongly clawed feet